BORN IN B

Geoff Ogden

Max Books

First published in the UK in 2020 by Max Books

A CIP catalogue record for this title is available from the British Library

ISBN: 978-0-9934872-7-9

Typeset and Design by Andrew Searle

Printed and bound in India

MAX BOOKS
2 Newbold Way
Nantwich
CW5 7AX
Email: maxcricket@btinternet.com
www.max-books.co.uk

In memory of Jack and Millicent

and

To Pauline, Sally, Simon, Jane and Sacha

and the rest of the family

Contents

Acknowledgements

The author would like to thank the following for their help and contributions: Malcolm Lorimer, Ken Grime, David Hodgkiss OBE, David Kaye, Jack Williams, Duncan Worsley, Oliver Worsley, Barry Howard, Sue McNeill, Mike Watkinson, Steve Edge, Paul Edwards, Matthew Parkinson, John Heaton, John Charlson, Gerry Wolstenholme, John Kay, Geoff Wellsteed, Lenny Kerr, Karl Krikken, Audrey Rushton, Martin Tebay, Colin Evans, Brian Krikken, Dave Fairbrother, Mark Nunn, Andrew Searle and Keith Hayhurst.

Photographs courtesy Lancashire C.C.C., David Kaye, Simon Pendrigh and Barry Mitchell unless stated.

Cartoons from Arthur Dooley.

The publisher wishes to thank David Hodgkiss OBE of William Hare for sponsoring the book.

Introduction

I was born in Stoneclough during the war in the house of Dr. T.B. Eames who was an avid Lancashire cricket supporter. He owned a full set of *Wisdens*, had seen W.G. Grace in action and had a cricket room upstairs full of memorabilia including a bat with which Ernest Tyldesley had scored a century. I was captivated from a very young age and he became a grandfather figure whose influence fostered my passion, some say obsession, for the game.

By the age of eight I was making regular visits to Old Trafford with his friends who included Jimmy Heap who lived in the village and was a former Lancashire player. I can clearly remember also travelling to Aigburth in 1949 to watch Lancashire play the New Zealand tourists only to find the gates had been closed. Such was the fervour for cricket at the time but visiting the nearby grave of 'The Child of Hale' was hardly recompense for the disappointment!

In 1950 I entered the junior department of Bolton School where I became friendly with Duncan Worsley who also lived on Green Lane, where we had moved to. When we were twelve we travelled by bus to the Parochial Church Hall, Astley Bridge for hour long coaching sessions with Charlie Hallows, the well-known Lancashire and England batsman. In our mid-teens we were playing first eleven school cricket and club cricket at Farnworth C.C. where our education was further developed by two good coaches Ron Booth and Jim Gledhill respectively.

I played for Farnworth in the Bolton League from 1954 to 1964 and the match that stands out most in my memory is the Hamer Cup final at Castle Hill in 1960. In a close game in front of almost 5,000 spectators we beat a very experienced and highly fancied Walkden team by three wickets with six teenagers in our side. We were very proud of our performance considering Peter Philpott was a last minute deputy professional for Walkden but Jim Gledhill's youth policy was that if you were good enough you were old enough and it paid off. There was a very strong Bolton School connection at Farnworth at the time as Duncan Worsley, Peter Jarvis, Roland Gee, Peter Boardman and myself all played together in the same school team that summer whilst the captain Alan Rushton, a future Mayor of Bolton, and professional Frank Hodgkiss were Old Boltonians. Graham Baxendale, who became a fine all-round cricketer, was the other teenager in the side.

In 1965 I joined Worsley C.C. in the Manchester Association and played there until I retired in 1985. I very much enjoyed my time there playing amongst many talented cricketers without quite the same cut throat competitive edge of the Bolton League. The highlight of my time there was winning the league in that glorious summer of 1976 when Duncan Worsley joined us for a season and another great friend and gifted batsman David Walker was captain. Only twelve months after retiring I was fortunate enough to be elected to the Lancashire C.C.C. Committee and a new chapter in my cricket career began.

I can remember vividly and with some trepidation my first General Committee meeting in 1986. I glanced around the table and there was Cyril Washbrook, Brian Statham and next to me Ken Grieves, my favourite batsman, bowler and fielder respectively when I was a junior member in the 1950s. It was decidedly one of those 'pinch yourself' moments but they were all friendly and welcoming once I got to know them better. It was just before the resignation of Chairman Cedric Rhoades and the start of a new era with Bob Bennett as Chairman and David Hughes as Captain for the 1987 season. A talented group of young players were beginning to emerge and the county was about to enjoy many one-day successes in the late '80s and early '90s. There were several hard luck stories regarding the Championship as we finished runners-up in 1987 and in three successive years from 1998-2000 and also in 2003 and 2006 but eventually the coveted trophy was secured in 2011. It was an ideal time to retire from the Committee and I had thoroughly enjoyed the experience.

The seeds of this book were sown when talking to Geoff Wellsteed a few years ago about his publication on cricketers born in Reading entitled *Inside The Boundary*. There was no doubt it was a very strong side, particularly in the batting department but I reckoned I could find a team from Bolton to rival it. In Peter May, Alec Bedser and Ken Barrington he had three great Test players but I argued my side had far more depth and variety not to mention twelve Test cricketers. After a few weeks of banter we shook hands and agreed to call it a draw.

I mentioned the 'Born In Bolton' team to Malcolm Lorimer who immediately suggested I should follow it up with a book. So here it is. Without his encouragement and expertise and the support of Ken Grime and David Hodgkiss I would not have gone ahead, but I have very much enjoyed the challenge and am extremely grateful to them all.

Geoff Ogden, February 2020

Geoff Ogden

Geoff and I have been great friends for over sixty years. We grew up in Bolton and attended Bolton School. At school Geoff was an absolutely outstanding sportsman as he was not only a fine cricketer but also an immensely talented footballer, playing for England Schools against Scotland Schools at Celtic Park and later gaining a Cambridge Blue. He was in addition very good at athletics, especially throwing the javelin.

Geoff Ogden coached by Charlie Hallows in 1953.

After completing his education Geoff became senior PE Teacher at Ellesmere Park Comprehensive School, married Pauline and became father to three children. At this time began his long connection with Worsley C.C., Lancashire C.C.C. and Lancashire youth cricket. Many of the players who have shone for Lancashire in the last thirty to forty years have passed through his representative teams.

Unfortunately a chronic hip condition led to Geoff's early retirement from teaching, two hip operations and a different direction in his life. He became a long standing and invaluable member of the Lancashire C.C.C. Committee, serving as Chairman of the Cricket Committee for many years. Throughout his life Geoff has made an enormously outstanding and selfless contribution to North West sporting life.

Duncan Worsley

Game in progress at Green Lane, the home of Bolton C.C. in July 1958.
(photo courtesy of the Bolton News)

Bolton cricket....why so prolific?

by David Kaye

When the *Bolton and District Cricket Association (BDCA)* celebrated its centenary in fine fashion in 1988, a key aspect of the milestone commemorations was the publication of the Association's history, entitled *Cotton Town Cricket*.

As well as claiming several 'uniques' and some 'notable firsts' for the BDCA, the book highlighted the prolific nature of the game in Bolton and neighbouring districts, comparing the town's 'summer sport scene' most favourably with other world cricketing 'hotspots', such as Bradford, Bombay (now Mumbai) and Barbados, and listing the names of a scarcely-credible 330 cricket clubs which had played under the auspices of the BDCA since its formation in 1888. Whilst this alphabetical list featured some clubs having played under more than one name, the net figure is no more than 20 fewer, and in the years since the centenary, an additional 11 clubs have swelled the list even further.

The vast majority of these clubs have been based within the various iterations of the Bolton borough boundary, although in latter decades, in the face of the many challenges facing league cricket generally, a significant number of clubs from adjacent districts (in the Greater Manchester boroughs of Bury, Trafford, Salford and Wigan) have been embraced, in order to maintain appropriate membership levels.

So, with such a huge number of cricket clubs within a relatively small compass in and around this Lancashire industrial town, the obvious question is *WHY?*

Whilst the reasons are manifold and complex, they essentially revolve around socio-economic aspects of life in the town in the Victorian and Edwardian eras, and given the space constraints of this overview, reference to the 3Ms - *Mills, Mines and Methodism* – may give some indication, albeit a considerably simplified one, of the origins of many of the clubs.

Due largely to the burgeoning cotton industry, Bolton grew extremely rapidly to become one of Lancashire's largest towns, and at its peak, a multiplicity of mills (weaving, spinning and bleaching) employed no less than 50,000 people. There was also a significant amount of coal mining in the district, and a substantial number of engineering enterprises.

As Bolton's urban sprawl expanded, the natural order of things meant that intense local rivalries developed between adjacent neighbourhoods, and indeed on an *inter-mill* and *inter-factory* basis. On an individual level, this rivalry manifested itself in the racing of pigeons, and the growing of the largest turnips, but on a 'group' basis it embraced activities such as brass banding, and, of course, encounters on the local football and cricket fields. Much of this was carried out on shoestring budgets, and in many cases, local patches of spare land (commonly known as *crofts*) were used for *both* summer and winter sports. As a result, many cricket pitches were at best *sporting*, and at worst *lethal*.

In Victorian times, leisure time in the industrial north of England was very limited indeed, with the workers having two primary 'destination options' available to them: the ubiquitous *alehouses*, or *places of worship*. Numerous churches and chapels of many different denominations had been built to meet the spiritual needs of Bolton's mainly working-class population, with many of these also providing education, and acting as *de facto* cultural, social and sporting hubs. Whilst the pubs scarcely registered on the scale when it came to fielding cricket teams, the town's places of worship had a huge impact. An analysis of the BDCA member clubs reveals that two thirds of that enormous number came from a combination of *churches* and the *corporate sector*, with mills, mines, tanneries, foundries and other industrial concerns accounting for 70, and 'Houses of God' no less than 130, of which 60 were attached to the disparate strands of Methodism.

Whilst historically renowned for exploiting the working classes, eventually some enlightened industrialists began catering for the needs of their workers beyond the factory gates, with a classic example of such philanthropy being the developments at Eagley Mills in 1837, when facilities for cricket and bowls were laid out, as well as the establishment of a library/reading room, and the formation of a brass band. Accordingly, today's Eagley C.C. proudly claims to be Bolton's oldest club, which was closely followed by Bradford Cricket Club in 1840, so-called because it was established under the patronage of the Earl of Bradford, who had an extensive estate in 'Bolton-le-Moors'. The name was short-lived, as the club metamorphosed into Bolton Cricket Club in 1846, after which it rapidly enjoyed great prestige, for many decades regarded as the town's premier cricket club.

Without doubt, the club was somewhat elitist, and if the many embryonic clubs of the town which rapidly followed Eagley could be regarded as being established for mill *workers*, Bolton C.C. was clearly a club for mill *owners*, and men of similar wealth, power and prestige in the town. Not for nothing were its members commonly known as 'Bowton Gents', and here we had something of a local microcosm of cricket's historic appeal across a broad spectrum of the social classes.

Such was the stature of Bolton C.C. that, during the 1860s and 1870s, it was able to stage a series of very prestigious matches, attracting to Bolton the most renowned cricket teams in the land, including *George Parr's All-England XI* (who played against '22 of Bolton'); *Manchester Cricket Club* (which metamorphosed into Lancashire C.C.C.); *United North* and *United South*. Of all these games, perhaps the most notable came in 1878, when the visitors were *United South*, captained by none other than W.G. Grace himself.

Not surprisingly, these games aroused great local interest, attracting large crowds, and added massive momentum to the development of cricket in Bolton.

Throughout the 1880s, there was much talk locally of the desirability of 'an organised cricketing body', perhaps partially influenced by parallel dialogue nationally within football, and the prospect of a professional football league. History was to determine that the *Bolton and District Cricket Association* was to be established in the same year as the *Football League*, with the inaugural meeting of the former held in *The Coffee Tavern* in Bradshawgate, Bolton, on 9th November 1888.

Bolton Cricket Club was to have a significant influence here as well, as two of its members, prominent local businessmen *Edward Cross* and *Samuel Isherwood*, each donated trophies (regarded as Lancashire's oldest), which provided great impetus in getting the embryonic Association up and running.

In its first season (1889) BDCA staged two knock-out competitions, *The Senior Challenge Cup* attracting 12 clubs, and *The Junior Challenge Cup* being contested by a further 34. Had league cricket been played in that first season, BDCA would have boasted the coveted title of 'The World's Oldest Cricket League', but disappointingly had to settle for the 'silver medal', since *The Birmingham and District League* (despite being constituted as an organised cricketing body several weeks after BDCA) staged a league competition from the outset.

The *Bolton Association* (as it was universally called thereafter) was an instant success, and was destined to expand just as rapidly as the town which spawned it. By the early years of the 20th century, BDCA comprised 65 clubs competing in 3 Divisions (with a total of 12 Sections), between them fielding a total of 110 teams every Saturday.

It is clear from contemporary reports that a key reason for the growth and success of BDCA was the excellence of its administration and progressive thinking, leading to the 'uniques' and 'firsts' mentioned earlier. Just one example of the Association's reputation for *ground-breaking innovation* was the introduction of paid neutral umpires at senior level.

As is so often the case, such rapid growth was not without its problems. The First Division had grown to 20 clubs by 1920, and this was considered totally unwieldy. Various formats were experimented with during the following decade, but none were deemed totally satisfactory, and discontent simmered amongst the 'elite' clubs, especially as all member clubs, irrespective of the paucity of their facilities, had equal voting rights. There were certainly some parallels with the scenario prevailing in the English Football League in more recent years, the result being that, in late 1929, twelve of Bolton's senior clubs announced they were to 'break away', and to form a new organisation to be known as *The Bolton Cricket League* (BCL), playing its first season in 1930.

(Understandably, in the wake of this 'seismic development', there was much residual ill-feeling, and what was frequently described as a 'cold war' between the two leagues prevailed for many years. Ultimately, there came the inevitable thaw in the relationship, and thankfully fierce but friendly competition between the two was ultimately to prevail. This was epitomised by the annual *Trinity Cup* competition (initially sponsored by a local paper mill) which was one of the most eagerly-anticipated dates in the local cricketing calendar from 1971 to 2015. Perhaps emphasising that the BCL had been formed by the town's 'elite' clubs, *t'League* was to dominate *th'Association*, with 30 wins against 12, with 3 games in the 45-match series being lost to rain.)

Thus it was that, for the next 85 years, Bolton was to boast *two* widely-respected senior cricket leagues, initially comprising 12 clubs each, with the Association continuing to have Second and Third Divisions for many years afterwards. Ultimately, BDCA increased its First Division to 14 clubs in 1975, with BCL doing likewise in 1984.

So, for the subsequent 30 years, cricket lovers in Bolton had the option of watching their cricket at no less than 28 different grounds, with each club having, in the time-honoured tradition of league cricket, one professional player, ranging in standard from outstanding local amateurs, to county players, to stars of *Test* and *One Day International* cricket. (The 2019 BCL handbook listed a total of 138 players who have represented their country at Test or ODI level, and whose talents have featured locally; whilst a similar list hasn't yet been compiled for BDCA, there has certainly been a fair representation of top international cricketers here as well.)

As in all aspects of life, nothing remains unchanged forever, and the league cricket scene in the north-west of England (and indeed elsewhere) has been more than a little turbulent for some years now, with many evolutionary, indeed *revolutionary*, changes. Again, the 'full story' is beyond the remit of this overview of Bolton cricket, but mention must be made of the advent of the *Greater Manchester Cricket League* (GMCL), with its 'pyramid' concept, as this has impacted significantly on our story.

History will be the ultimate arbiter with regard to the degree of success of this venture, but it is most regrettable that several cherished cricket leagues, all well over 100 years old, have fallen by the wayside as a result, including our own Bolton and District Cricket Association, whose last season (of a total of 127, as BDCA was one of the very few leagues which played throughout both world wars) was 2015.

Several clubs from both BCL and BDCA opted to join GMCL, and in an effort to protect its own future, BCL announced an ambitious plan to increase membership from 14 to 24 clubs, with a view to a future two-division set-up, with 12 clubs in each, and promotion and relegation. This further depleted the ranks of the BDCA, with the result that, with only seven remaining clubs, a league competition was no longer viable, and most of these clubs were embraced into BCL (in 2016), which currently has a membership of 20, in two groups of 10, known as the *Premier Division* and the *Association Division*, the latter being a sop to history.

Despite this turmoil, Bolton cricket remains very vibrant, with ever-increasing standards both on field and off, and recent innovations, clearly influenced by the first-class game, including the highly popular T20 competition, played on Friday evenings. But in many respects, the most heartening aspect, despite the perennial challenges, is the strength of cricket at junior level, with most clubs fielding teams at under 9, 11, 13, 15 and 18 age groups.

As long as this situation prevails, there should be no reason why cricket clubs in Bolton will not continue to supply a constant stream of exciting talent to Old Trafford (and indeed, to other counties too), and we feel sure that the impressive list of first-class players born in Bolton, the inspiration for this fascinating publication, will continue to expand well into the future...

In conclusion and further emphasising what a hot-bed of cricket the Bolton district has long been, in addition to the two *senior* leagues, there have been two *junior* organisations which have contributed significantly for many years, and certainly merit brief mention:

Horwich Sunday School Cricket League was formed in 1922, and whilst for many years membership was confined to church-based teams, over the years it became increasingly difficult to sustain a league comprised entirely of such, so the organisation evolved into *Horwich Churches and Welfare Cricket Association*, embracing clubs from a diversity of sources, including schools, companies, and even pubs! Although currently struggling for membership, over the years over 40 clubs have played their cricket under this banner, the vast majority being from the Horwich district, augmented by a few participants from Chorley and Wigan.

Formed in 1958, *Bolton Cosmopolitan Cricket League* catered for players only able to participate in mid-week, and again comprised mainly school, college, corporate and 'scratch' teams, with many of the games played on the grounds of BCL and BDCA clubs. Fortunes have fluctuated in recent years, with membership varying between 8 and 14 clubs, but the BCCL was given a major fillip in 1991, when BDCA disbanded its Second Division, and donated the relevant trophies to the Cosmopolitan League. With its ranks significantly swollen by the former BDCA member clubs, BCCL secured some valued commercial sponsorship, and re-structured, forming two divisions.

So, a final thought: Having attempted to profile Bolton as a *unique cricketing town* for various reasons, perhaps an additional claim to fame results from its *four* cricket leagues, which, whilst perhaps contrasting starkly in levels of proficiency, facilities etc., have all contributed positively in their own way to produce some 'golden threads' for such a wonderfully-rich cricketing tapestry.

David Kaye, Blackrod, Bolton - February 2020
President/Life Member, Lostock Cricket Club
(Members of Bolton Cricket League, Premier Division)

Bolton - A Stronghold Of Cricket

by Jack Williams

Bolton and its immediate surroundings have long been a stronghold of cricket. The numbers playing cricket each week during the summer months have probably been as high as those for any other town in Lancashire or the rest of northern England. For most of the 1920s more than 3,000 paid each week to watch the highest level of cricket in the Bolton area but this figure ignores the numbers of club members who did not have to pay to watch matches or those watching the lower levels of cricket. Cricket coverage in the *Cricket and Football Field* which became titled *The Buff* in 1916, the Saturday sports edition of the *Bolton Evening News*, was more extensive than that of their equivalents in other Lancashire towns and no doubt reflected and stimulated interest in cricket. For most of the twentieth century cricket encouraged social cohesion in the Bolton area. In the districts adjoining Bolton County Borough such as Eagley, Bradshaw, Egerton, Horwich, Farnworth, Little Lever, Westhoughton and Kearsley, supporting the leading local clubs expressed and helped to consolidate localised loyalties. Support for clubs playing at the highest levels of local cricket often crossed class boundaries as players were recruited from the middle and working classes while wealthy businessmen patronised clubs. Much of men's cricket was dependent on the co-operation of their women folk who helped to prepare match teas, supported club cash raising events and accepted that men could be freed from domestic duties to give them the time to play cricket. No doubt some would call this a form of female exploitation and some men may have stopped playing cricket because of pressure from their wives. On the other hand, interviews in the1980s with women whose husbands had played cricket in the middle decades of the twentieth century often said that their husbands could have done much worse than play cricket and mentioned that wives enjoyed socialising with other wives when helping clubs.

One distinction of league cricket in Bolton and its surroundings is that since the 1890s they have been the only town in Lancashire to sustain a high-status league. The other leading leagues in Lancashire were regional organizations with clubs from several towns and larger industrial villages. Nearly all the clubs in the Liverpool Competition were from, or close to, Liverpool but for much of the twentieth century it had no formal organisation and its clubs denied that it was a league.

As in so much of the industrial North and Midlands, most teams playing cricket from the 1890s on a regular basis in the Bolton area were participating in leagues whereas before the 1960s only the humblest clubs in the South of England tended to play in leagues. Bolton had a key role in the establishment and growth of league cricket in Lancashire, which has always been regarded as a bastion of league cricket. The Birmingham League which began playing in 1889 was the first cricket league established in England. It seems highly likely that this was stimulated by the success of the Football League's first season in 1888-89. The Bolton and District Association had been formed in 1888. It held two knock-out competitions in 1889 and started its league, cricket's second league to be formed, in 1890. When the BDCA collapsed before the 2016 season, it could boast of having played league cricket continuously for longer than any other cricket league in the world. The Birmingham Cricket League had not played during the First World War. The BDCA kick-started league cricket in Lancashire. The Lancashire League and the Central Lancashire, usually regarded as the most prestigious cricket leagues during the twentieth century in Lancashire, were both formed in 1892. By 1900 there were still clubs in Lancashire that played only friendly matches but in most towns the great majority of clubs which played regularly were playing in leagues. By 1900 84 teams were playing each week in the eight sections of the BDCA. While it has to be conceded that if the BDCA had not formed its cricket league, the example of the Football League and of the Birmingham Cricket League would have probably led to the creation of a league elsewhere in Lancashire, but had the BDCA's venture not succeeded, the spread of league cricket in Lancashire could have been slower.

In the early twentieth century the First Division of the BDCA was seen as one of the leading leagues of Lancashire. During the 1920s the stronger First Division clubs began to feel that expanding the Division to twenty clubs had been a mistake and in the winter of 1929-30 twelve of the strongest clubs resigned from the BDCA to form the Bolton League which immediately became regarded as one of the premier leagues in Lancashire and clearly superior to the First Division of the BDCA. Until the very recent past, the Bolton League never quite equalled the eminence of the Lancashire and Central Lancashire Leagues but it was not far behind them. During the past five years economic difficulties provoked a major restructuring of the higher levels league cricket in the North West. The Bolton League appeared to have emerged stronger from these changes which were disastrous for the BDCA. In 2016 the BDCA collapsed after it lost senior clubs to the newly created Greater Manchester Cricket League. Two clubs left the Bolton League for the Greater Manchester league but nine clubs from BDCA were admitted to the Bolton League which was then able to have Premiership Division and an Association Division. Dramatic changes affected the Lancashire and Central Lancashire Leagues. In 2016 the Central Lancashire League and the Saddleworth League merged to form the Pennine League but this disbanded in 2017 when seven clubs from what had been the Central League were admitted to the Lancashire League. The remaining seventeen clubs from the Pennine League joined the Greater Manchester League. It will be interesting to see whether the prestige of the Bolton League soon matches that of the Lancashire League.

Bolton was also a stronghold of church-based cricket clubs. In the first half of the twentieth century it was always among the cotton towns with the highest proportions of clubs based on churches, chapels or Sunday schools. The peak was perhaps reached in 1900 when 97 out of 111 teams were connected with places of worship. The number of church teams was lower in the 1920s and 1930s but still formed above 40 per cent of all teams. Numbers dropped further after the Second World War. The decline of church teams can be seen as a sign of growing secularisation but an even more potent factor could have been that church clubs were usually too poor to own their grounds and many grounds were sold for housebuilding. A club usually collapsed when its ground was sold. Oral evidence collected in the 1980s with those who played for church clubs in the 1930s shows that church teams played cricket in a fiercely competitive manner but they tended to encourage church attendance and strengthened assumptions about cricket playing helping to consolidate Christian morality.

Bolton was strongly represented in the increasing numbers of workplace cricket teams in the first half of the twentieth century. In 1914 the Bolton area had only three workplace teams playing each week but by 1939 probably had at least as many as any area in Lancashire outside the cities of Liverpool and Manchester and their immediate surroundings. Because of financial support from works managers and the small sums collected each week from employees, works sports clubs often had better facilities than independent or church clubs. Employers may have thought that subsidising sport for employees could discourage animosity to employers among workers; it is also possible that sports enthusiasts among workers may have urged employers to provide sports facilities. As in the rest of industrial Lancashire, the closure of cotton factories and the decline of mining had hit workplace cricket clubs hard in the second half of the twentieth century.

Given the great enthusiasm for cricket in India, Pakistan and Bangladesh, it is not surprising that the migration of South Asians to Bolton added a further dimension to Bolton cricket. During the last quarter of the twentieth century Asians in Bolton began to form clubs reflecting different strands of Asian society in the area. Clubs were based on ancestral villages in South Asia, different religious groups or districts in Bolton. Bolton Indians emerged as the strongest club with a predominantly Hindu membership while the Deane and Derby club came to be the most successful Muslim club. There were reports of complaints from Asians that no predominantly Asian club had been admitted to the Bolton League whereas clubs from outside Bolton had been admitted. More recently it would seem that more players of Asian descent are playing for Bolton League clubs. It is perhaps appropriate to note that the two most recently Bolton-born cricketers to have played for England are of Asian descent.

One of the strongest reasons for seeing Bolton and its surroundings as a stronghold of cricket is that the number of its natives who have played first-class cricket is probably higher than that for any other town. This in itself is a tribute to the vitality of Bolton cricket and deserves to be celebrated alongside all that the area has contributed to cricket. Geoff Ogden, Ken Grime, Malcolm Lorimer and David Kaye are to be congratulated on the depth of their research and for making such a valuable addition to the social history of cricket in England.

Action from Bolton v Broughton at Green Lane in July 1968.
(photo courtesy of the Bolton News)

Qualification Criteria

Players who qualify to be included in my *Born In Bolton* team must have been born in the Metropolitan Borough of Bolton and played first-class cricket for a county. The list of players is based solely on my research and I do not claim it to be definitive. There are inevitably some excellent cricketers who were brought up in the Bolton League or Bolton Association who do not qualify on grounds of birth such as Ronnie Irani (Leigh), Colin Hilton (Atherton) and Steve O'Shaughnessy (Bury).

I had to draw a line somewhere, however, as the architects of the metropolitan system did in 1972 and there is an interesting story relating to that decision. Worsley is situated in an area which would easily have merged with either Bolton, Wigan or Salford and there had to be a casting vote on the final decision by the Chairman of Worsley Urban District Council who chose Salford. If it had been Bolton, in my opinion a much better fit, two of Lancashire's greatest batsmen, J.T. Tyldesley and Ernest Tyldesley, who were born in Roe Green and played for both Roe Green and Worsley cricket clubs, would have qualified for selection. Incidentally, it is not generally known that the sister of the two highest run scorers in Lancashire's history was the great grandmother of Michael Vaughan, who was born in Eccles. His father Graham played for Worsley C.C. for many years and Michael, along with his brother David, attended St. Mark's Junior School, Worsley as J.T. and Ernest had done in the past. Interestingly, there is a blue plaque on the wall of Roe Green Independent Methodist Church commemorating the fact that all three of these famous cricketers were baptized there. Sadly the Vaughan family moved to Sheffield when Michael was eight and although he travelled to Old Trafford for trials in his mid-teens he signed for Yorkshire, making his debut aged eighteen. He had inherited the Tyldesley genes however through his mother Dee and soon became a classy opening batsman in county and Test cricket and one of England's most successful captains.

Metropolitan Borough of Bolton

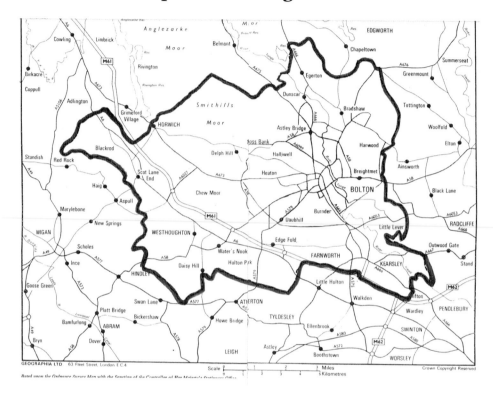

EDITOR'S NOTES:

All statistical information is correct as of 1st March 2020.

Biographical details refer to a player's appearances for Lancashire unless otherwise stated.

The Players

Walter Hardcastle

RHB/RF
b. 10th February 1843, Great Bolton
d. 27th April 1901, Bolton
Career 1869-1874, 4 matches
Debut v Sussex, Old Trafford, 24th June 1869
HS: 11 v Sussex, Old Trafford, 1869
Did not bowl

WALTER MITCHELL HARDCASTLE was born in Bolton on 10th February 1843. He was a middle order right hand batsman who played regularly for Bolton C.C. and also represented Lancashire in four matches between 1869 and 1874. His county debut was against Sussex at Old Trafford where he scored 0 and 11 and he was not invited to appear again until 1873 when he totalled 13 runs in four innings against Surrey at The Oval and Kent at Gravesend. Lillywhite's Annual for 1874 noted that *"with more confidence would be a valuable man to his county; bats in good form and drives well."* His final first-class score was 9 in his only innings against Derbyshire at Chesterfield in 1874.

Perhaps the highlight of his cricketing days was the game in which he scored 21 and 6 for '18 of Bolton C.C.' at Green Lane against the United South of England under the captaincy of W.G. Grace in 1878. He did not make many runs but he could at least claim he was dismissed by the great man in each innings. However that is not really surprising as Grace bowled unchanged throughout the match delivering 70 overs and taking 20 wickets for 130 runs.

When the 1881 census was taken three years later Hardcastle was living at the York Hotel on Newport Street in Bolton where his mother was the publican, and he was employed as a draughtsman in an iron foundry. He died on 27th April 1901 aged 58.

Inns	Runs	HS	Ave	50/100	Balls	Runs	Wkts	BB	Ave	5w/10w	Ct
7	33	11	4.71	0/0	-	-	-	-	-	-	1

Frank Hardcastle

b. 12th May 1844, Firwood
d. 5th November 1908, London
Career 1869, 2 matches
Debut v MCC, Lord's, 19th July 1869
HS: 9 v Surrey, The Oval 1869
Did not bowl

FRANK HARDCASTLE was born in Firwood, Bolton on 12th May 1844. He was the fourth son of James Hardcastle of Firwood Hall, Bolton and eventually became head of Thomas Hardcastle & Son, bleachers and dyers, which had been established by his grandfather at Firwood in 1803.

Coming from a wealthy family Hardcastle was educated at Repton School where he played as a batsman for the cricket team in 1861 and 1862. In 1865 he was selected for the Gentlemen of Lancashire against the Gentlemen of Yorkshire at York where he scored 13 not out and 8 and followed with 8 not out and 16 against the Players of Lancashire at Whalley, both matches finishing as low-scoring draws. The following year he is known to have played for Twenty-Two of Bolton against an All England Eleven at the Back o' th' Bank ground with the 'Twenty-Two' losing by an innings after totalling just 44 all out and 62 all out, Hardcastle making 6 and 1. In July 1867 he was selected for the Gentlemen of Lancashire again for their match against the Gentlemen of Yorkshire at Old Trafford, scoring 31 in an innings dominated by E.B. Rowley's 219 and Edwin Whittaker's unbeaten 146 in a total of 586.

Hardcastle is also at the centre of a mystery regarding his appearances for Lancashire C.C.C. In 1867 he is thought to have made his debut for the county in the three-day Roses match at Middlesborough on 2nd and 3rd September (the scheduled third day was not required as Yorkshire won easily) under the name 'J. Jackson' making 3 in each innings. The anecdote passed down through the years to historians at Old Trafford was that J. Jackson was actually Frank Hardcastle playing under an assumed name, although nobody appears to know the reason why. The 1868 *Wisden* has J. Jackson shown in their scorecard of the match while *Scores and Biographies* has Hardcastle playing in the game but a note underneath their scorecard of the match states: *"another version of the score has J.Jackson playing instead of F.Hardcastle"*. To muddy the waters further website *Cricket Archive* has J. Jackson listed on their scorecard of the match as another person altogether, John Wilson Jackson, brother of Lancashire player Edward Jackson. What is not in dispute is that the day after the Middlesborough match was due to end, Hardcastle played at York for the Gentlemen of Lancashire against the Gentlemen of Yorkshire making 10 and 11. Arthur Appleby is the only player known for certain to have played in both games. So who did play at Middlesborough-Hardcastle or 'Jackson'? We may never know for sure.

Hardcastle played further games for the Gentlemen in 1867 and 1868 before being selected for two Lancashire matches on their mid-summer trip to London to play MCC and Surrey in July 1869. He met with little success scoring 2 not out and 6 in the match at Lord's-but could boast he had competed against the great W.G. Grace - followed by a duck and 9 at The Oval. He never played first-class cricket again and retired to concentrate on business matters.

He became the proprietor of Breightmet Collieries, Bolton, entered politics as M.P. for Westhoughton from 1885 to 1892 and was appointed High Sheriff for the County of Lancashire in 1895-96. He also maintained his interest in cricket as he became the first President of the Bolton & District Cricket Association from 1889 to 1892. He moved to London where he died from heart failure on 5th November 1908 aged 64 at his home in Lancaster Gate.

Inns	Runs	HS	Ave	50/100	Balls	Runs	Wkts	BB	Ave	5w/10w	Ct
4	17	9	5.66	0/0	-	-	-	-	-	-	1

George Winder

RHB
b. 16th July 1850, Bolton
d. 1st February 1913, Ottery St Mary, Devon
Career 1869, 4 matches
Debut v MCC, Lord's, 19th July 1869
HS: 22 Gentlemen of the North v Gentlemen of the South,
Lillie Bridge, West Brompton 1871
Did not bowl

GEORGE ALEXANDER WINDER was born at Ainsworth House, Bolton on 16th July 1850. He was educated at Rossall School and played in the school cricket and football elevens. In the 1870 *Lillywhite's Companion* he is described as having: *"safe and pretty defence, can always be depended on for runs; splendid field; good slow bowler."*

He was only 5ft. 4 inches tall and weighed just over 9 stone and shortly after leaving Rossall the right handed batsman played two matches for Lancashire in July 1869 against M.C.C. at Lord's and Surrey at The Oval scoring 23 in his four innings. The following July he played for the Gentlemen of Lancashire against the Gentlemen of Warwickshire, opening the batting with Sam Swire and scoring 39 and 31, and he also took four wickets. He played against the Gentlemen of Warwickshire again the following season at Warwick, scoring 33 in his only innings.

In 1871 he played two further first-class matches; for the Gentlemen of the North, scoring 12 and 22 in an innings defeat to the Gentlemen of the South at Lillie Bridge, West Brompton and, having gone up to Christ's College, Cambridge, one game for the University team scoring 3 and 4 not out against Surrey at The Oval.

In January 1872 he badly damaged his left hand in a shooting accident and it had to be amputated. He continued to play cricket however and, after gaining his degree, became land agent for Sir J.H. Kennaway in Ottery St. Mary, Devon. He died there in 1913 aged 62.

Inns	Runs	HS	Ave	50/100	Balls	Runs	Wkts	BB	Ave	5w/10w	Ct
8	64	22	8.14	0/0	-	-	-	-	-	-	1

Thomas Rushton

b. 14th May 1845, Moor Platt, Horwich
d. 1st July 1903, Garstang
Career 1870, 1 match
Debut v Hampshire, Old Trafford, 21st July 1870
HS: 7 v Hampshire, Old Trafford, 1870
Did not bowl

THOMAS HENRY RUSHTON was born at Horwich on 14th May 1845. As a teenager he played for Bolton C.C. when they played at the Back-o'-th'-Bank ground and was one of the club's best batsmen, particularly strong on the leg side. On 23rd-25th August 1866 he played for Twenty-two of Bolton against the All England XI, scoring 5 and 0 and on 5th-7th August 1869 he played for Twenty-two of Bolton against the All England XI making 30, the top score for his side.

In 1870 he was selected for the Lancashire team against Hampshire at Old Trafford and scored 7 in his only innings batting at number seven. It was the first fixture against Hampshire and Lancashire won comfortably by ten wickets with A.N. Hornby scoring a magnificent 132.

In the history of Lancashire cricket, however, the match has become famous for the fact that Bill Hickton took all ten wickets in Hampshire's second innings. This was the first occasion that a Lancashire bowler had achieved this feat and Hickton's 10 for 46 remains the best-ever analysis for the county. The only other Lancastrians to take all ten wickets in an innings are Johnny Briggs with 10 for 55 against Worcestershire at Old Trafford in 1900 and Bob Berry with 10 for 102 also against Worcestershire at Blackpool in 1953.

Rushton became head of the well-known local firm Dobson & Barlow Limited, Bolton who were textile machinery manufacturers. He was the eldest son of Thomas Leven Rushton, who was Mayor of Bolton from 1848 to 1850, and became a J.P. in later life. His residence was at Halliwell Hall, Bolton before he moved to the Barnacre Estate, near Garstang in 1881. He died rather suddenly of a perforated appendix in Garstang on 1st July 1903 aged 58.

Inns	Runs	HS	Ave	50/100	Balls	Runs	Wkts	BB	Ave	5w/10w	Ct
1	7	7	7.00	0/0	-	-	-	-	-	-	-

RG Barlow

RHB/LM
b. 28th May 1851, Barrow Bridge
d. 31st July 1919, Blackpool
Career 1871-1891, 351 matches
Debut v Yorkshire, Bramall Lane, 17th July 1871
HS: 117 v MCC, Lord's 1885
BB: 9-39 v Sussex, Old Trafford 1886
Tests: 17, 1881/82-1886/87
HS: 62 v Australia, Sydney 1881/82
BB: 7-40 v Australia, Sydney 1882/83

RICHARD 'DICK' GORTON BARLOW was born at Barrow Bridge, Bolton on 28th May 1851 and cricket was the absorbing passion of his life. He was totally obsessed by the game and frequently played truant, or feigned illness, in his early school days in order to practise his favourite game instead. He made his own bats and balls and with his older brother Robert would challenge other boys to a game for a penny or twopence. They were unbeatable and soon found that nobody would play against them! Consequently Barlow resorted to lengthy practice, batting 15 minutes at a stretch and reluctantly giving up his bat when it was another boy's turn.

When he was eleven years-old Barlow carried his bat through an innings for 14 runs in a school match between St. George's and All Saints. Two years later he repeated the feat, scoring 33, in another school match at Bolton Park and for good measure also took a hat-trick. Barlow accomplished these feats batting left-handed, his natural choice, but remarkably at this point he switched to batting right-handed for the rest of his life on his father's advice.

Occasionally, when school was over, Barlow would go to the cricket ground at Tonge Moor where the 'Bolton Gents'-the name given to the premier Bolton club at that time-were at practice. For twopence or

Inns	Runs	HS	Ave	50/100	Balls	Runs	Wkts	BB	Ave	5w/10w	Ct
608	11217	117	20.61	39/4	43481	13799	950	9-39	14.52	66/14	268

threepence he would then do the necessary fielding required and thus met some 'fine cricketers' including Frank Hardcastle, Walter Hardcastle and William Scott, who all played for Lancashire around this time.

Having moved to Derbyshire with his family in 1865 Barlow showed great promise when representing Staveley against George Parr's All England team and was advised by William Hickton-the first Lancashire bowler to take all ten wickets in an innings-to approach the county for a trial. He did not follow Hickton's advice, preferring to accept professional terms at Chesterfield and then Farsley, near Leeds. From this point he learned a great deal about accepting the responsibilities of both batting and bowling before being selected to represent Lancashire at the age of 20, without a trial, in 1871. His debut at Sheffield was a success despite breaking a finger while batting at number 7 on the opening day. He returned with his hand bandaged on the second morning on the fall of the ninth wicket and helped Arthur Appleby add 64 runs for the last wicket, contributing 28 not out, before Appleby was bowled when on 99. Brought on to bowl on the third morning because of a stubborn 82-run stand for the 9th wicket Barlow promptly bowled Johnnie West and thus became the first Lancashire bowler to take a wicket with his first delivery in first-class cricket. Yorkshire followed-on shortly afterwards and Barlow took three more wickets as the Red Rose triumphed later that day by ten wickets.

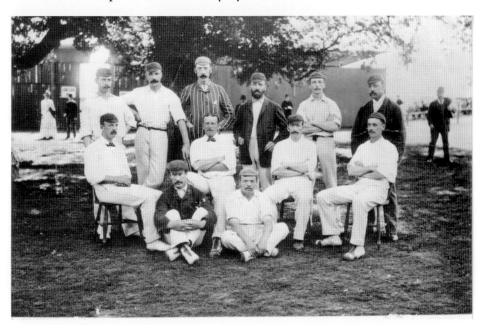

Lancashire in the early 1880s with Barlow standing third from right and AN Hornby seated second left.

Barlow was without doubt one of the greatest all-rounders of his era. *Wisden* even stated in 1883: *"He is fairly entitled to be reckoned the best all-rounder cricketer in England."* As a batsman he possessed great technical ability and concentration, relying heavily on the forward defensive stroke. He was most definitely the archetypal, cautious opening batsman, a perfect foil for his partner A.N.Hornby who was aggressive and displayed a cavalier approach to the game. His obdurate batting is best illustrated by the fact that he carried his bat in 11 innings for Lancashire and not one was a century. Charlie Hallows is next on the list and he achieved the feat on six occasions. It was Barlow's innings of 5 not out in two and a half hours when he opened the batting against Nottinghamshire in 1882 that gave birth to the term 'stonewaller'. Billy Barnes, one of the Notts' bowlers, said after the innings: 'Bowling at thee were like bowling at a stone wall.'

Barlow bowled slow/medium left arm in a most miserly fashion with both accuracy and variety, yet it was 1878 before he was a recognised bowler. In 1885, for example, he bowled for an hour against Sussex conceding just a single and recorded the following outstanding analyses for Lancashire; 5 wickets for 3 runs v Kent in 1878, 6 for 3 v Derbyshire in 1881, 5 for 10 v Gloucestershire in 1884 and 9 for 39 in his best-ever performance against Sussex in 1886.

Outside Test cricket the best performance of his career was for the North v Australia at Trent Bridge in 1884 when he scored a century on a poor pitch against the fired-up Fred Spofforth and he took 10 wickets for 48 runs in the match. In addition to his batting and bowling skills he was also a brilliant fielder who specialised in the point area.

In considering Barlow's achievements in his seventeen Test appearances it is important to remember he played against Australia every time and that pitches were sometimes rather unpredictable. His batting average was 22.73 and he only scored two half-centuries but often he occupied the crease and fought hard for runs when most needed. On paper his bowling achievements appear more impressive, starting at The Oval in 1882 where he took 5 for 19 in 31 four-ball overs whilst the following year he recorded 7 for 40 at Sydney. He also enjoyed great success on his home ground in 1886 when, after decent scores in each innings with the bat, he routed Australia in their second innings taking 7 for 44 in 52 overs to assure victory. His outstanding feat is recorded on the Test Match Honours Board in the Long Room at Old Trafford whilst in the same room he is also depicted in a splendid stained glass window alongside his captain A.N.Hornby and wicketkeeper Richard Pilling. All three Lancastrians played in the first Test Match to be staged at Old Trafford in 1884.

Barlow retired from first-class cricket in 1891 but continued to play in the leagues. He had proved himself to be an outstanding cricketer but he had also been involved in athletics and football to a very high standard, acting as referee in the famous FA Cup match in 1887 when Preston North End beat Hyde 26-0. He became a dealer in sports goods for a time before settling in a large house in Blackpool which housed his collection of memorabilia. He even designed his own gravestone which stands in Leyton Cemetery near Blackpool and contains the inscription: "Bowled At Last". Barlow died at Stanley Park, Blackpool on 31st July 1919.

It would be remiss to end without mentioning that Barlow, alongside his opening partner A.N.Hornby, are immortalised in the famous cricketing poem written by Lancastrian Francis Thompson called 'At Lord's', which ends:

> *"As the run stealers flicker to and fro,*
> *To and fro:*
> *O my Hornby and my Barlow long ago!"*

William Scott

b. 1845, Bolton
d. 17th June 1899, Queen's Park, Bolton
Career 1874, 1 match
Debut v Kent, Old Trafford, 17th July 1874
HS: 9 v Kent, Old Trafford 1874
Did not bowl

WILLIAM AINSLIE SCOTT was born in Bolton in 1845-his actual date of birth is unknown-and he played for Bolton C.C. at the original ground at Back-o-th'-Bank. In 1874 he played one first-class match for Lancashire against Kent at Old Trafford batting in the middle order and scoring 9 and 5 not out.

He was, however, involved in a much more interesting game later in his career when Bolton C.C. moved to their new ground at Green Lane. He was invited to play for Bolton C.C. against The United South of England captained by W.G. Grace in 1878 with the proceeds going to charity. These were the early days of Test cricket and there were two future England players in the United South team, namely W.G. and G.F. Grace. Only two years later they would be joined by a third brother, E.M. Grace, in the England team that beat Australia by five wickets at Kennington Oval in the first Test on English soil. W.E. Midwinter, who opened the batting with 'W.G.' in this particular game, had already played for Australia in the first-ever Test against England at Melbourne in 1876. Rather surprisingly Midwinter, who was born in Gloucestershire, had been persuaded by 'W.G.' to change allegiance and he made his debut for England against Australia at Melbourne in the 1881-82 series. He immediately created a record in becoming the only cricketer to have represented Australia in England and England in Australia. The fourth participant at Green Lane who was already a Test player was James Southerton who had represented England twice against Australia at Melbourne C.C. in 1876 at the age of 49. He is still the oldest player to make his Test debut, a record that will surely stand for ever.

Returning to the match at Green Lane, Scott only scored 9 and 18 and was caught off W.G.Grace's bowling in each innings, but I am sure he would have enjoyed the rare experience of playing in such illustrious company and in front of a large and receptive crowd. It is almost irrelevant, but Grace's team won the game by 21 runs at lunchtime on the third day yet were obliging enough to play an exhibition match in the afternoon.

A draughtsman at Hick, Hargreaves and Co in Bolton, Scott became manager of Messrs J.B.Holden and Co, wine and spirit merchants of Deansgate and Oxford Street, Manchester in 1888 and became one of the partners in the business in 1893.He retained his interest in Bolton Cricket Club and was a leading light in the organisation of fund-raising bazaars for the club. Early in 1898 he caught typhoid fever and, although he appeared to recover, his health was seriously undermined. He eventually succumbed to peritonitis on the morning of Saturday 17th June 1899, at his residence at 171 Chorley New Road, Bolton.

Inns	Runs	HS	Ave	50/100	Balls	Runs	Wkts	BB	Ave	5w/10w	Ct
2	14	9	14.00	0/0	-	-	-	-	-	-	-

Joseph Kevan

b. 13th September 1855, Bolton
d. 9th December 1891, Queen's Park, Bolton
Career 1875, 2 matches
Debut v Kent, Old Trafford, 26th July 1875
HS: 12 v Kent, Catford 1875
Did not bowl

JOSEPH HENRY KEVAN was born in Bolton on 13th September 1855. He was a keen cricketer and joined Bolton C.C. playing in the first match staged at the new Green Lane ground on 10th July 1875. The opponents were Lancashire C.C. Club & Ground with whom Bolton had regular fixtures and on this particular occasion the famous Lancashire bowler Alec Watson was a member of the team. Bolton made a very creditable score of 193 with Kevan hitting a dashing 92, and it was this innings that most likely led to the nineteen year-old being selected for Lancashire against Kent a couple of weeks later. He played in only two county matches, both against Kent. In the first at Old Trafford he batted at number ten and made a pair whilst in the return match at Catford he completed a hat-trick of ducks, batting at nine, before being sent in to open in the second innings and scoring 12 of the 18 runs required for victory.

His father and brother were both chartered accountants and Joseph chose to follow the same profession. Sadly he died very young at Queen's Park, Bolton on 9th December 1891, aged 36.

Inns	Runs	HS	Ave	50/100	Balls	Runs	Wkts	BB	Ave	5w/10w	Ct
4	12	12	3.00	0/0	-	-	-	-	-	-	-

Abraham Brooks

b. 29th May 1852, Darcy Lever, Bolton
d. 7th May 1925, Breightmet Fold, Bolton
Career 1877, 1 match
Debut v Yorkshire, Fartown, Huddersfield, 12th July 1877
HS 6 v Yorkshire, Fartown, Huddersfield, 1877

Wicketkeeper ABRAHAM WORTHINGTON BROOKS was born in Darcy Lever on 29th May 1852. He played for Bolton C.C, Farnworth C.C. and Darcy Lever C.C. and on 25th and 26th May 1877 played at Old Trafford for XVI Colts of Lancashire against Manchester C.C. where he opened the batting scoring 0 and 7.

His only first-class appearance followed two months later in the July 'Roses' match at Fartown, Huddersfield. Batting at number 10 he made 6 in his only innings and took two catches in Yorkshire's second innings as Lancashire won by nine wickets. In a season where Lancashire used five different wicketkeepers in their 11 matches it appears Brooks was called up to play because the more regular 'keeper Edward Jackson was not available. Then in the match following the Roses victory Lancashire gave a debut to 21-year-old Dick Pilling who would quickly establish himself behind the stumps and progress to playing eight times for England.

Instead Brooks continued to play club cricket and featured in a number of 'Great Matches' against touring teams. In July 1878 he played in the match between 'Eighteen of Bolton Cricket Club' against the United South of England at Green Lane. On that famous occasion the visitors were captained by W.G. Grace and although Brooks batted at No.3 in both innings, he didn't distinguish himself. He was caught off the bowling of 'W.G.' for 7 in the first innings, and only scored 6 in the second innings, but at least had the satisfaction of catching Grace in the United South's second innings. In June 1879 he played for XVIII of Farnworth against the United London XI and scored 9 and 13 and the following month for XXII of Chorley against the United North of England scoring 6 and 0 and making one stumping.

Brooks is also known to have played in the second-ever B.D.C.A. Cross Cup final in August 1890 where he opened the batting for Darcy Lever, scoring 15, and is referred to in a press report as being: 'the old Bolton wicket-keeper'. Darcy Lever's opponents were Eagley, who triumphed in an exciting and low scoring game by two runs (106 all out v 104 all out).

Inns	Runs	HS	Ave	50/100	Balls	Runs	Wkts	BB	Ave	5w/10w	Ct/St
1	6	6	6.00	0/0	-	-	-	-	-	-/-	2/0

18 of Bolton v United South of England Eleven

**Venue: Green Lane, Bolton on 18th, 19th, 20th July 1878
Result: United South of England Eleven won by 21 runs
Umpires: J May, W Mortlock**

United South of England Eleven

	First innings		Second innings	
WG Grace	c Birmingham b Tranter	51	c Brooks b Mills	22
WE Midwinter	c Brooks b Shooter	12	b Bembridge	4
EH Butler	c Blackburn b Tranter	3	b Bembridge	1
HRJ Charlwood	b Tranter	0	b Bembridge	63
GF Grace	b Tranter	12	c Howarth b Mills	1
WR Gilbert	b Tranter	26	c Brooks b Mills	12
M Riley	c Mills b Tranter	7	b Mills	0
R Humphrey	b Bembridge	9	not out	6
R Fillery	b Tranter	0	c and b Mills	0
FL Butler	not out	5	b Mills	0
J Southerton	b Bembridge	1	run out	5
Extras	(7 b, 2 lb, 1 w)	10	(3 b, 3 lb)	6
Total	(all out)	136	(all out)	120

Bolton first innings

	First innings		Second innings	
R Blackburn	b WG Grace	6	b Southerton	0
S Birmingham	c Fillery b WG Grace	17	b WG Grace	1
AW Brooks	c Humphrey b WG Grace	7	c Midwinter b Southerton	6
H Wall	b WG Grace	8	b Southerton	5
WA Scott	c GF Grace b WG Grace	9	c Fillery b WG Grace	18
E Mills	c Midwinter b WG Grace	0	b Southerton	0
E Tranter	b Southerton	5	lbw b WG Grace	4
WM Hardcastle	b WG Grace	21	c FL Butler b WG Grace	6
TT Holt	c Midwinter b Southerton	22	c Fillery b WG Grace	2
A Entwhistle	b WG Grace	4	c WG Grace b Southerton	5
T Shooter	c WG Grace b Southerton	1	st Midwinter b WG Grace	0
JA Brown	b WG Grace	5	b Southerton	2
H Bembridge	c Fillery b WG Grace	21	c GF Grace b WG Grace	9
WT Dixon	c [unknown] b WG Grace	0	not out	12
C Howarth	b Southerton	1	c GF Grace b WG Grace	8
GH Crook	st Midwinter b WG Grace	2	run out	6
H Brown	st Midwinter b Southerton	4	b Southerton	0
W Johnston	not out	0	retired hurt	7
Extras	(3 b, 1 lb)	4	(7 b)	7
Total	(all out)	137	(all out)	98

Note: The fall of wickets and bowling figures are not known

Joseph Hewitson

LHB/SLA
b. 27th October 1865, Little Bolton
d. 4th December 1925, Halliwell, Bolton
Career 1890, 4 matches
Debut v Oxford University, Old Trafford, 19th June 1890
HS: 56 v Middlesex, Old Trafford 1890
Did not bowl

JOSEPH HEWITSON was born in Little Bolton on 27th October 1865. He was a very promising slow left arm bowler and useful middle order left hand bat who initially played for Bolton C.C. before making his Lancashire debut against Oxford University at Old Trafford in 1890 as deputy for the injured Johnny Briggs. He enjoyed immediate success against the inexperienced students, taking 6 for 57 and 4 for 58. This was by far his best first-class bowling performance as he only took 4 wickets for 120 runs in his three County Championship games and scored 84 runs with a top score of 56 in four innings. In his final match against Gloucestershire at Old Trafford in 1890 he somehow upset both W.G. and E.M. Grace and never played for

1885-86 Season
(With the Bolton Charity Cup, The Lancashire Cup and the Derby Charity Cup)
(Back) Bentley, Weir, Hutchinson, Trainer, J.Parkinson(1), Roberts, J.Parkinson,(2), J.Parkinson(3)
(Front) Davenport, Brogan, Steele, Struthers, Hewitson, Hough

Lancashire again. He returned to Bolton C.C., played for Lancashire League side Burnley C.C. in 1893-94 and was signed by Eagley C.C. as professional in 1900.

Hewitson was also a talented footballer who played on the left wing for Bolton Wanderers in the days before league football started although he appeared subsequently in at least 3 recorded League games and scored 3 goals. In 1885 he scored the only goal against Blackburn Rovers in the Lancashire Cup Final at Deepdale as Bolton won the oldest trophy in the English game.

He died at Halliwell, Bolton on 4th December 1925 aged 60.

Inns	Runs	HS	Ave	50/100	Balls	Runs	Wkts	BB	Ave	5w/10w	Ct
5	99	56	19.80	1/0	571	235	14	6-57	16.78	1/1	1

James Hallows

LHB/LMF
b. 14th November 1873, Little Lever
d. 20th May 1910, Farnworth
Career 1898-1907, 139 matches
Debut v MCC, Lord's, 9th May 1898
HS: 137 * v Middlesex, Old Trafford 1904
BB: 9-37 v Gloucestershire, Gloucester 1904

JAMES 'JIMMY' HALLOWS was born in Little Lever, Bolton on 14th November 1873 and as a youngster played for the local Temperance Cricket Club before joining Little Lever C.C. He immediately proved to be a talented cricketer which attracted the attention of the County Club and he was invited to represent Lancashire Colts in a trial match at Old Trafford in 1896. Against some good bowlers he scored 133 and 77 not out to impress the county coach so much that he was quickly pencilled in as a player of the future. He was duly invited to join the Manchester C.C. groundstaff for the 1897 season.

Hallows was a stylish, free flowing left handed batsman and initially a fast medium left arm bowler who, on the advice of former Lancashire player Sydney Crosfield, changed to medium/slow which proved to be a success. He was also an excellent fielder but his weakness was that he suffered from ill health. In a match against Yorkshire in 1905 he had to be carried from the field by fellow players after an attack of epilepsy.

Hallows' debut was against M.C.C. at Lord's in 1898 but it was not until 1901 that he became a regular member of the side scoring 1,000 runs for the first time, including his maiden century and taking 35 wickets. He was again effective in the following season with 776 runs and 49 wickets but his best summer was undoubtedly 1904 when his all-round ability was instrumental in Lancashire winning the Championship for the first time since 1897.

HEAP.   CUTTELL.   KERMODE.   TYLDESLEY.   HALLOWS.   SLADEN.   SHARP.

LANCASHIRE CRICKET TEAM. (Professional.)

James Hallows (third from right) with the Lancashire professionals
who helped secure the 1904 County Championship.

The general outlook was not optimistic as the 1904 season started without the great Sydney Barnes who, after taking 131 wickets the year before, had decided to play in the Lancashire League. Although the batting was strong the bowling appeared to lack penetration, but such gloomy predictions were confounded when Hallows, placed in a position of responsibility, bowled very skilfully to claim 108 wickets. He received substantial support from Willis Cuttell, a slow/medium leg break bowler, who took exactly 100 wickets and pacemen Walter Brearley and Alex Kermode who took 77 and 65 wickets respectively. In the batting department Johnny Tyldesley with well over 2,000 runs and Reg Spooner with 1,664 runs were outstanding while Hallows also reached the 1,000 run mark. Furthermore the side could also count on runs when needed from the likes of Jack Sharp, Les Poidevin, Archie MacLaren, A.H. Hornby and Cuttell. In the end Lancashire enjoyed one of the best seasons ever and were unbeaten in the County Championship with 16 wins and ten draws. They were, by far, the best team in the competition and second-placed Yorkshire only managed to win nine games.

Hallows had played a major role in winning his only Championship medal and he had also completed the 1,000 runs/100 wickets 'double' on the last day of the season. In doing so he joined Cuttell as the second Lancashire player to achieve the feat, and only Len Hopwood in 1934 and

1935 has reached the same level since. Why only three Lancashire players have completed the double is something of a mystery. Nevertheless Hallows fully deserved to be named one of *Wisden's* 'Five Cricketers of the Year' in the 1905 annual.

That Championship-winning season established Hallows as one of the finest all-rounders in the country and greatly enhanced his reputation. He had promised to be an outstanding cricketer from his early days at Old Trafford as hopeful comparisons to Johnny Briggs were mentioned and even the great C.B. Fry reported in one match that he had "illustrated his cricketing genius". The sad fact remains that Hallows had to constantly struggle with poor health and although he played well to reach 763 runs at 42.88 in 1905, his bowling swiftly deteriorated and he was never able to repeat the high standards of his golden summer. We will never know what heights he may have reached if he had been more robust.

At the end of the 1907 season Hallows announced his retirement with a career record of 5,065 runs at 28.77, including eight centuries, and 287 wickets at 23.26 each. Sadly his condition never improved and he died prematurely on 20th May 1910 at the age of 36. He was buried in Farnworth Cemetery.

Inns	Runs	HS	Ave	50/100	Balls	Runs	Wkts	BB	Ave	5w/10w	Ct
203	5065	137*	28.77	23/8	16694	6677	287	9-37	23.26	14/5	57

Walter Brearley

RHB/RF
b. 11th March 1876, Bolton
d. 30th January 1937, Marylebone, Middlesex
Career 1902-1921, 134 matches
Debut v Sussex, Hove, 11th August 1902
HS: 38 v Northamptonshire, Old Trafford 1908
BB: 9-47 v Somerset, Old Trafford 1905
Tests: 4, 1905-1912
HS: 11 not out v Australia, Kennington Oval 1905
BB: 5-110 v Australia, Kennington Oval 1905

WALTER BREARLEY was born in Bolton on 11th March 1876 before moving to Derbyshire with his family where he was educated at Tideswell Grammar School. As a young man he returned to his native county and played for various teams including Farnworth Parish Church C.C., Bolton C.C. and Bury C.C. before impressing the coaches and fellow cricketers whilst representing Manchester Cricket Club.

Brearley was no batsman but he had a good build and terrific attitude for a fast bowler. He was strong and sturdy and possessed the stamina that enabled him to bowl just as fast and enthusiastically in the evening session as he had done in the morning. He made his maiden first-class appearance for Lancashire against Sussex at Hove in 1902 and although his figures were unimpressive he had at least made a start.

In 1903 Brearley began to make his mark as a top-class pace bowler taking 69 wickets as he learned to swing the ball with both accuracy and bounce from a short run-up. In one game both he and Sydney Barnes took ten wickets each in the victory against Surrey at Old Trafford while his 6 for 81 against Yorkshire in his first Roses match, also at Old Trafford, was further proof of his rapid progress.

The following season saw Brearley capture 95 wickets in helping Lancashire to win the County Championship outright for the third time but it was in 1905 that he really excelled with 133 victims at an average of 19. Against Somerset at Old Trafford he had match figures of 17 for 137, including four wickets in four balls, which was later bettered by Harry Dean with 17 for 91 against Yorkshire at Aigburth in 1913. They remain the only two bowlers to have taken more than 16 wickets in a first-class game for Lancashire. In the tourist match against Australia, Brearley impressed further by capturing 7 wickets for 115 including such fine players as Clem Hill, Monty Noble and Syd Gregory. Lancashire overwhelmed Yorkshire in the Roses game at Old Trafford in front of a crowd of almost 25,000 with Brearley once more rising to the occasion in taking 5 for 31 in the first innings. In the return fixture at Sheffield he continued his good run of form with a match analysis of 13 for 157. Brearley's consistent success eventually impressed the England selectors and he was chosen to play in the last two Tests against Australia at Old Trafford and The Oval. He proved to be up to the mark with figures of 4 for 72 and 4 for 54 on his home pitch and 5 for 110 at The Oval including taking the wicket of the great Victor Trumper on three occasions.

In 1906 Brearley only played five matches and none at all in 1907 after falling out with the Committee. Although he was a likeable character he could be impulsive, resigning on more than one occasion only to return when he cooled down. The club was always more than ready to welcome him back however as he was a match-winning bowler and very popular with the supporters. He did in fact reappear in 1908 and was in great shape taking 148 wickets in the Championship. In selecting Brearley as one of their 'Five Cricketers of the Year' *Wisden* stated there was no cricketer playing who had a 'more marked individuality'.

Brearley continued his good form in 1909 taking 118 wickets with a season's best of 9 for 80 against Yorkshire, a team that he particularly enjoyed playing against having captured 125 wickets in fourteen Roses games. He was again selected for England against Australia at Headingley along with four fellow Lancastrians; J.T. Tyldesley, Jack Sharp, A.C. MacLaren and Sydney Barnes. Brearley bowled with some credit taking 3 for 78 in 38 overs.

After two unremarkable summers Brearley left Lancashire at the end of the 1911 season although he played for England once more while representing Cheshire, but was given little opportunity against South Africa at Lord's in 1912 as England won easily by an innings. The county had lost a fine bowler and the supporters would miss a wonderful entertainer. They loved it when he made his entrance as a batsman by vaulting the pavilion gate and rushing to the middle, often without his gloves. His appearance when Lancashire were bowling was also notable and impressive as described by Neville Cardus: "the first impulsive stride of Brearley as he took the field with the rest of the Lancashire eleven was enough of itself to whisk somebody's hat high into the air; the blusterous confidence of the man hit you smack in the face and made your blood tingle". In short, his brisk walk to the middle signified he meant business and the crowd and the opposition knew it.

In later life Brearley kept in touch with cricket by coaching at Lord's for several years. He died at Marylebone in January 1937 at the age of sixty and was laid to rest at Bowness in the Lake District. He will be fondly remembered alongside the likes of Johnny Briggs and Cec Parkin as one of the great characters of Lancashire cricket.

Inns	Runs	HS	Ave	50/100	Balls	Runs	Wkts	BB	Ave	5w/10w	Ct
185	908	38	5.89	0/0	29500	16305	844	9-47	19.31	93/27	52

John Bullough

RHB/SRA
b. 1893, Bolton
d. 3rd June 1967, Westhoughton
Career 1914-1919, 8 matches
Debut v Nottinghamshire, Trent Bridge, 11th June 1914
HS: 17 v Middlesex, Old Trafford 1914
BB: 5-123 v Derbyshire, Derby 1914

JOHN BULLOUGH was born in Bolton in 1893 (actual date unknown) and played in four matches for Lancashire in 1914 and four more immediately after the 'Great War' in 1919. He was a lower order right hand batsman and right arm slow bowler who was selected for Lancashire's Second Eleven match against Yorkshire Second Eleven at Old Trafford in August 1913, and he made his first team debut in 1914 against Nottinghamshire at Trent Bridge. He bowled economically throughout the game with match figures of 5 for 128 in 66 overs and even outbowled the far more experienced spinner Jimmy Heap. It was a decent start but the highlight of his first-class career was against Derbyshire at Derby where he completed a hat-trick and recorded his best figures of 5 for 123 as Derbyshire amassed 524 in their only innings.

After the war matches in 1919 were played over two days and Bullough was unable to make an impact, so he left Old Trafford at the end of the season having taken 13 wickets for 573 runs at 44.07 and scored 24 runs at an average of 4.80. He continued to play league cricket for several clubs including Leyland Motors, Atherton, Horwich and Westhoughton. He died on 3rd June 1967 at Westhoughton.

Inns	Runs	HS	Ave	50/100	Balls	Runs	Wkts	BB	Ave	5w/10w	Ct
8	24	17	4.80	0/0	1344	573	13	5-123	44.07	0/0	3

Charlie Hallows

LHB/LMF
b. 4th April 1895, Little Lever
d. 10th November 1972, Bolton
Career 1914-1932, 383 matches
Debut v Yorkshire, Hull, 23rd July 1914
HS: 233 * v Hampshire, Aigburth 1927
BB: 3-28 v Northamptonshire, Old Trafford 1914
Tests: 2, 1921-1928
HS: 26 v West Indies, Lord's, 1928

CHARLES HALLOWS was born into a cricketing family in Little Lever, Bolton on 4th April 1895. His father and grandfather had played for the local village team and it was in the Bolton Association, playing for Little Lever C.C., that Hallows began to make his mark in the game. His uncle, the gifted all-rounder Jimmy Hallows, played for Lancashire and was the first player to complete the 'double' for the Red Rose county in 1904. Charlie, as he was generally known, was brought to the attention of the county club and was engaged at the age of 18 in 1913, making his maiden appearance in a friendly game against Yorkshire in 1914 just before the start of the Great War. He was called up serving in the King's Liverpool

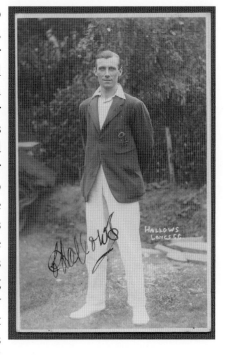

Regiment and was not demobilised until May 1919 when he was swiftly re-engaged by his native county.

Considering he had not played any serious cricket for four years Hallows made a spectacular start to his first-class career in 1919 by scoring three consecutive centuries in matches against Sussex at Old Trafford, Yorkshire at Sheffield and Nottinghamshire at Old Trafford. By the end of the season he had accumulated 1,000 runs for the first time, an achievement he repeated in eleven successive years between 1919 and 1929. It is interesting to note that the 1919 season was unusual in that all county games were restricted to two days with extended hours of play, with the result being determined by the percentage of actual wins to matches played. Unsurprisingly almost half were draws and it was quickly decided to return to three days of play in 1920.

In 1921, after scoring three early season centuries and 227 against Warwickshire, Hallows was selected for England against Australia in the fourth Test at Old Trafford. In a rain-affected match he did not bat in the first innings and scored 16 not out in the second but the game was drawn although not without incident as the Australian captain Warwick Armstrong breached the laws of the game when, after a delay in proceedings, it was

realised that he had bowled two overs consecutively. Hallows only played in one more Test, against the West Indies at Lord's in 1928, scoring 26 in his only innings in which he opened with the great Herbert Sutcliffe. Many less talented batsmen have represented England in far more Tests but Hallows was rather unfortunate in that his career coincided with the likes of Sutcliffe and Jack Hobbs in their prime years.

Hallows was tall, dark and handsome and cut an impressive figure on the field of play. During his career he was involved in many successful opening partnerships with Harry Makepeace initially, and then Frank Watson, both of them right handed and basically defensive batsmen who were difficult to dislodge. Hallows, on the other hand, was left handed, elegant and a graceful straight driver and had the ability to mix both defence and attack depending on the situation. All three were essential to Lancashire's success in winning three consecutive County Championship titles in 1926-27-28 as they laid the foundations necessary to gain control of matches.

The two most successful and satisfying seasons so far as Hallows was concerned must have been in 1927 when he scored 2,119 runs with a best-ever average of 73.06 and was chosen as one of *Wisden's* 'Five Cricketers of the Year', and 1928 when, as well as winning a third successive Championship medal, he became one of only three batsmen ever to score 1,000 runs in May. This magnificent achievement took just 27 days from 5th May to 31st May and, having made 190 not out on 30th May against Sussex at Old Trafford, he needed 42 more runs on the final day to achieve his target. In the end he reached 232 somewhat nervously and by doing so joined two legends of the game in W.G.Grace and Wally Hammond. After celebrating and relaxing at last he was promptly caught next ball! By the end of the season he had amassed his best aggregate of 2,564 runs exceeding Frank Watson by only 23 runs and Ernest Tyldesley by 97 runs. No wonder Lancashire won the title that year! It was the first time that three Lancashire players had exceeded 2,000 runs in the same year and has only been equalled by Ken Grieves, Geoff Pullar and Alan Wharton in1959.

Undoubtedly one of Lancashire's best ever opening batsmen Hallows retired in 1932 with a proud record. Overall he scored 20,956 first-class runs at an average of 40.24 with 55 centuries including eleven hundreds in his glorious summer of 1928. For a time he continued to play league cricket before being appointed Chief Coach at Worcestershire initially and then Lancashire. On returning to Old Trafford he lived on Bradford Road, Great Lever and died suddenly on 10th November 1972 at the age of 77 after complaining that he was out of breath.

Inns	Runs	HS	Ave	50/100	Balls	Runs	Wkts	BB	Ave	5w/10w	Ct
586	20926	233*	40.24	94/55	1583	750	19	3-28	39.47	0/0	142

Dick Tyldesley

RHB/SRA
b. 11th March 1897, Westhoughton
d. 17th September 1943, Over Hulton
Career 1919-1935, 397 matches
Debut v Northamptonshire, Northampton, 4th June 1919
HS: 105 v Nottinghamshire, Old Trafford 1922
BB: 8-15 v Northamptonshire, Kettering 1926
Tests: 7, 1924-1930
HS: 29 v South Africa, Headingley 1924
BB: 3-50 v South Africa, Lord's 1924

RICHARD KNOWLES TYLDESLEY, commonly referred to as Dick, was born in Westhoughton on 11th March 1897. His father was a Westhoughton club cricket professional who coached his four sons to play the game successfully but Richard, although the youngest, turned out to be the most gifted. All four were on the Lancashire groundstaff at one stage or another but should not be confused with the Tyldesleys from Roe Green, John Tommy and Ernest, who were two of the greatest batsmen ever to represent Lancashire, each scoring over 30,000 runs in first-class cricket.

As a young boy Tyldesley practised constantly in the nets learning how to spin and flight the ball and vary his pace and length. Although nominally a leg break bowler he was not a great spinner of the ball but kept the batsmen guessing as he used the top spinner with considerable success. The county club became aware of his skilful bowling at Westhoughton C.C. and after trials at Old Trafford in 1919 he was offered a contract. He made his county debut against Northants and at the end of the season had captured 33 wickets at 21.72 each. Tyldesley had made a promising start which continued in 1920 and 1921 with 61 wickets at 21.16 and 78 at 19.12 respectively and moreover he had demonstrated he was no mean batsman and possessed a safe pair of hands.

Tyldesley became an indispensable member of the Lancashire bowling attack during the golden years of the 1920's. In the early part of the decade the portly, seventeen stone Tyldesley teamed up with the tall, dark and good looking Cec Parkin to create a very successful spin double act that provided skill, variety and deception and no little comedy on occasions. During this period Yorkshire were very strong and won the Championship in four consecutive seasons from 1922 to 1925 but it was soon to be Lancashire's turn at the top as Parkin retired and was replaced by the dynamic Ted McDonald who, with his express pace, joined the tireless Tyldesley to form

Dick Tyldesley with Cec Parkin (left) and Ted McDonald (right)

a different but nevertheless devastating type of partnership. Their success together was a major factor in Lancashire winning the Championship title in 1926, 1927, 1928 and 1930.

In his first-class career Tyldesley claimed 100 wickets in ten successive seasons from 1922 to 1931, a feat bettered only by Johnny Briggs who reached the target on eleven occasions but not in consecutive years. He was undoubtedly most successful in the summer of 1924 when he claimed 184 wickets in all matches and delivered many outstanding performances. The season started incredibly well as Lancashire thrashed the South African tourists at Old Trafford in May with Tyldesley taking 12 for 78 in the match. In early June he claimed 6 for 18 in an astonishing Roses victory at Leeds as Yorkshire were dismissed for 33 to lose by 24 runs. In the match at Old Trafford against Leicestershire he took five wickets without conceding a run whilst at Aigburth against Northants he claimed seven wickets for six runs. He was selected for England in four of the five Tests against South Africa and acquitted himself well taking six wickets at Lord's and bowling economically throughout the series. His reward for such an outstanding season was to be selected as one of *Wisden's* 'Five Cricketers of the Year' in the 1925 Almanack.

He gathered 1,449 wickets at 16.65 each in his career for Lancashire which is only exceeded by Briggs, Brian Statham and Arthur Mold. In 1929 he took four wickets in four balls against Derbyshire at Derby to join George Nash

DICK TYLDESLEY.

and Walter Brearley in the Lancashire record books. He was a useful batsman scoring over 6,000 runs at 15.78 with one century against Nottinghamshire at Old Trafford in 1922 and he also held 322 catches. He played in 7 Tests and although he was fairly successful in four matches against South Africa in 1924 and was selected in A.E.R. Gilligan's side to tour Australia in 1924/25 he was not a success on bone-hard pitches and played in only one Test at Melbourne. His final two England games were against Australia at Trent Bridge and Headingley in 1930 and he recorded overall Test figures of 19 wickets for 619 runs at 32.57 and 47 runs at an average of 7.83.

After a dispute with Lancashire regarding his contract he left the club at the end of the 1931 season and returned to league cricket where he reckoned he could make more money for less work. He helped Nantwich C.C. to win the North Staffs & District League twice in successive years and then moved to Accrington C.C. in 1934. He died at Over Hulton on 17th September 1943 when he was only 46 years old and it is a sad fact that not one of his three brothers managed to even reach that age.

Inns	Runs	HS	Ave	50/100	Balls	Runs	Wkts	BB	Ave	5w/10w	Ct
464	6419	105	15.65	15/1	66759	25980	1509	8-15	17.21	101/22	334

Alf Hall

LHB/LFM
b. 23rd January 1896, Bolton
d. 1st January 1964, Johannesburg, South Africa
Career 1920/21-1930/31, 46 matches
Debut: Transvaal v Griqualand West, Johannesburg, 16th December 1920
HS: 22 Transvaal v MCC, Johannesburg 1923
BB: 8-80 Transvaal v Natal, Johannesburg 1926
Tests: 7 (for South Africa), 1922/23-1930/31
HS: 5 v England, Cape Town 1922/23
and 5 v England, Johannesburg 1927/28
BB: 7-63 v England, Cape Town 1922/23

ALFRED EWART HALL was born in Bolton on 23rd January 1896 and emigrated to South Africa with his family as a baby. When he was ten years old he returned to Bolton on a short trip and played some local cricket finding no difficulty in taking wickets in boys matches. On one occasion he completed a hat-trick and impressed a spectator so much that he interrupted the game and presented him with two pennies. Hall never forgot it.

Returning to South Africa Hall continued to develop as a tall, left-arm medium fast bowler and was eventually selected to play for Transvaal in 1920. The South African captain Herbie Taylor admired his performances for Western Provinces against the MCC and also in the Currie Cup matches for Transvaal, especially when he captured twelve

Reproduced by permission of "The Star" Johannesburg.
A. E. Hall.

wickets in a victory over Natal at Johannesburg. Taylor was convinced he was good enough to play Test cricket and Hall made his maiden appearance against England at Newlands on New Years' Day 1923. In the first innings he took 4 for 49 and in the second, with England needing 173 runs to win, bowled magnificently to dismiss seven batsmen for 63 as England scraped home by one wicket. For his outstanding effort he was carried shoulder high from the field by his team-mates. He played in the three remaining Tests of the series which England won by two matches to one, producing another fine analysis of 6 for 82 in the fourth Test in Johannesburg.

Reproduced by permission of "The Star," Johannesburg.

At the start of the 1923 English season Hall was tempted to try his luck in Championship cricket with Lancashire, his native county, and joined Werneth C.C. After much deliberation the MCC refused his registration as he had played for Transvaal, the equivalent of a county, in the same year. Instead Hall played four first-class matches for Lancashire against Oxford and Cambridge Universities in May, the touring West Indies in June and The Rest at Blackpool in September, taking 6 for 23 against Oxford University on his Red Rose debut and eight wickets in the following match against the Cambridge students.

His registration was accepted for the following season and Hall returned to mix league duties with three Championship appearances and two matches for Lancashire against the touring South Africans at Old Trafford and Liverpool. It was not a resounding success. In his first match against Glamorgan, who had joined the County Championship the season before, Hall only bowled in the second innings, taking 2 for 25, as the visitors were skittled for just 22 and 107 at Aigburth. In the next match he watched on again as South Africa were shot out for 60 at Old Trafford by Cec Parkin and Dick Tyldesley before he went wicketless from 13 overs when the tourists batted a second time, while Parkin and Tyldesley wreaked havoc once more to bowl the tourists out for 155. By contrast the second tour match against South Africa at Old Trafford was a high-scoring draw with both sides batting once, Hall opening the bowling with Ted McDonald but failing to take any of the three wickets to fall. Further Championship appearances against Nottinghamshire and Worcestershire yielded just one wicket and that was the end of his association with Lancashire.

Hall decided to return to Transvaal and his success back in South Africa earned a recall to the Test team against England in the 1927/28 season. He was immediately effective taking 6 for 100 and 3 for 67 in beating England at Johannesburg but he failed to take a wicket at Durban as South Africa won to square the series. In his final Test against England at Johannesburg in 1931 he took 4 for 105 in a drawn game to finish with 40 Test wickets overall at 22.15 each and a very high strike rate of almost six wickets per match.

At first glance it appears rather surprising that Hall only played in seven Tests, all of them against England, but it may be related to the fact that every match was in South Africa on matting pitches. He died aged 67, on New Years' Day 1964 in Johannesburg exactly 41 years after his Test debut.

Inns	Runs	HS	Ave	50/100	Balls	Runs	Wkts	BB	Ave	5w/10w	Ct
57	134	22	3.72	0/0	11175	4502	234	8-80	19.23	21/6	13

Bill Farrimond

RHB/WK
b. 23rd May 1903, Daisy Hill
d. 15th November 1979, Westhoughton
Career 1924-1945, 153 matches
Debut v South Africa, Aigburth, 16th July 1924
HS: 174 Minor Counties v Oxford University, The Parks 1934
BB: 0-16 v South Africa, Aigburth 1935
Tests: 4, 1930/31-1935
HS: 35 v South Africa, Durban 1930/31

IT WAS RATHER unfortunate for Bill Farrimond that his Lancashire career coincided so closely with that of George Duckworth. They were both outstanding wicketkeepers who were very different in character. Duckworth was aggressive, ebullient, a great motivator and loud appealer, very much one of the great characters of his era, while Farrimond was almost the complete opposite, quiet, modest and content to display his technical skills unobtrusively. There is no doubt that Farrimond was a better batsman than Duckworth, which did not matter so much in those days as it does now, but Duckworth's superior craftsmanship behind the stumps ensured he was always the preferred selection.

William (Bill) Farrimond was born at Daisy Hill, Westhoughton on 23rd May 1903 and initially played at Daisy Hill C.C. before moving to Westhoughton C.C. He was offered a contract at Lancashire in 1924 and made his first-class debut against South Africa at Liverpool in July of that year. During his career which basically lasted sixteen years, he only played for the first team on 134 occasions but he nevertheless managed to represent England in four Tests and was considered by some good judges to be the second best wicketkeeper in the country. Not only did he reach the heights of Test cricket he also equalled the existing record of dismissals by a wicketkeeper worldwide when he claimed seven victims in an innings against Kent at Old Trafford in 1930. The record had previously been held by E.J. Smith of Warwickshire and it has since been broken but it still stands as a

Lancashire record which has been equalled more recently by Warren Hegg against Derbyshire at Chesterfield in 1989 and Luke Sutton against Yorkshire at Headingley in 2008.

Farrimond's introduction to Test cricket was on the South African tour of 1930-31 when ironically Duckworth was ill and he replaced him in the fourth Test in Johannesburg and the fifth Test in Durban. His other two Tests were against the West Indies at Port of Spain and South Africa at Lord's, both in 1935, and overall he acquitted himself well, scoring 116 runs at 16.57 and claiming seven victims as wicketkeeper. Uncomplainingly he returned to Lancashire to play mainly Minor Counties cricket in the Second Eleven and it was not until Duckworth virtually retired that he was able to take his place on a regular basis for the 1938 and 1939 seasons. He slotted seamlessly into the role but sadly,after two satisfying years, the Second World War intervened and he would never play County Championship cricket again.

County cricket was suspended during the war and Farrimond, who lived in Westhoughton, decided to return to his former club in the Bolton League. He was immediately installed as captain and under his shrewd guidance Westhoughton C.C. became league champions for the first time in 1940. As a bonus he finished at the top of the league batting averages and one former player stated that he could never be described as elegant but he was strong on the leg side and skilful in finding gaps in the field. He continued to lead the side to victory in 1941 and 1942 as Westhoughton completed a hat-trick of titles with his friend and neighbour Dick Pollard the professional on both occasions. Two very talented local lads had returned from county cricket to bring much needed joy and satisfaction to their former club and supporters.

When the war ended in 1945 county cricket slowly came back to life but the County Championship did not resume until the following year. Farrimond had played some friendly matches for Lancashire in 1945 but decided not to continue full time at the age of 42. His first-class record for Lancs was 2,202 runs at an average of 21.17 and 297 victims as wicketkeeper. He had played only two full seasons for the first team and we will never know what he might have achieved if he had taken up other offers of more first-class cricket at other counties. Farrimond had quite simply enjoyed playing for his native country and will be long remembered as a fine wicketkeeper and one of the most loyal players ever to wear the red rose. He died in Westhoughton at the age of 76 on 15th November 1979.

Inns	Runs	HS	Ave	50/100	Balls	Runs	Wkts	BB	Ave	5w/10w	Ct/St
168	2908	174	23.64	16/1	18	16	0	0-16	-	0/0	252/80

Frank Rushton

RHB/RFM
b. 21st April 1906, Little Bolton
d. 15th October 1975, Queen's Park, Bolton
Career 1928-1929, 6 matches
Debut v Hampshire, Old Trafford, 14th July 1928
HS: 28 v Leicestershire, Aigburth 1929
BB: 4-30 v Gloucestershire, Old Trafford 1929

FRANK RUSHTON was a tall fast-medium seam and swing bowler who had the ability to bowl accurately and vary his pace skilfully. He was born in Bolton on 21st April 1906 and started to play cricket at Kearsley C.C. in the Bolton Association where he attracted the attention of the County Club who offered him a contract for the 1928 and 1929 seasons.

He turned out regularly for the Second Eleven in his first season taking 40 wickets at 14.85 and also proving he was a useful batsman with 323 runs at 26.91 with a top score of 84. He was selected to play for the full County side on three occasions taking 3 wickets for 160 runs but the following summer showed some improvement, especially in the match against Gloucestershire where he opened the bowling with Ted McDonald and recorded figures of 0 for 27 from 27 overs in the first innings and 4 for 30 in the second including the wickets of two Test players, Alfred Dipper and a young Charlie Barnett. Sadly that was to be his best performance as he was not re-engaged for the 1930 season, a decision that was surprising to several local cricket reporters. He left the first-class game with a record of 10 wickets at 36.20 and 59 runs at 11.80 in his six appearances.

In 1930 Rushton signed professional terms at Royton C.C. in the Central Lancashire League and remained there for three years. He then moved to Bolton C.C. for one year where he had a good season with both bat and ball persuading local club Eagley C.C. to sign him as professional for what turned out to be the next 17 years. It was an inspired choice as Rushton's arrival signalled an upturn in fortunes for the club. During his long reign Eagley won their only three League Championships and reached three Hamer Cup finals winning once. He left Eagley at the end of the 1950 season with an amazing record having captured 1,444 wickets including 10 wickets in an innings on three occasions. He moved to Little Lever as professional for a further two years before retiring in 1952 at the age of 46 with 1,561 wickets to his name in the Bolton League, a record that has only recently been surpassed.

In retirement Rushton loved to watch his son Alan, a former Farnworth C.C. captain and future Mayor of Bolton, playing cricket at his old club Eagley and even in his fifties he would often be tempted to take off his jacket and bowl in the practice nets. He was without doubt one of the best bowlers to grace the Bolton League, greatly respected both on and off the field. He died in his beloved Bolton at Queen's Park on 15th October 1975 aged 69.

Inns	Runs	HS	Ave	50/100	Balls	Runs	Wkts	BB	Ave	5w/10w	Ct
5	59	28	11.80	0/0	1098	362	10	4-30	36.20	0/0	2

Dick Pollard

RHB/RFM
b. 19th June 1912, Westhoughton
d. 16th December 1985, Westhoughton
Career 1933-1952, 298 matches
Debut v Nottinghamshire, Old Trafford, 19th August 1933
HS: 63 v Derbyshire, Old Trafford 1947
BB: 8-33 v Northamptonshire, Old Trafford 1947
Tests: 4, 1946-1948
HS: 10 * v India, Old Trafford 1946
BB: 5-24 v India, Old Trafford 1946

RICHARD 'DICK' POLLARD was born in Westhoughton, near Bolton on 19th June 1912. He played his early cricket at Daisy Hill C.C. in the Bolton Association and at the age of 17 was a member of the first team which won the Isherwood Cup in 1929. His early promise was rewarded by the offer of a Lancashire contract for the 1933 season.

Pollard was a big, heavy man with a barrel chest who bowled fast/medium from a long and lumbering approach to the wicket. He was one of the most accurate and reliable bowlers on the circuit who had the ability to bowl seamers and outswingers, and he would continue for over after over without complaint. It was hardly surprising he was given the nickname 'th'owd chain horse'. He was very popular with team-mates and supporters alike, an ordinary Lancashire lad who gave everything he had and was just happy to be earning a living playing a sport he loved.

He made his debut in August 1933 against Nottinghamshire taking the wicket of England Test player Arthur Carr as his first victim. In the Championship-winning team of 1934 he played in eleven matches, taking 38 wickets at 19.31 with an outstanding performance of 6 for 21 against

Gloucestershire at Old Trafford. In the following season Lancashire dropped to fourth in the Championship but Pollard made good progress, playing in 23 matches and capturing 100 wickets in first-class cricket for the first time. He had made a strong statement and for the next four summers up to the start of the war he continued to reach the 100-wicket target.

County cricket was suspended during the war and Pollard returned to the Bolton League as a professional at Astley Bridge before fulfilling the same role at his local club Westhoughton C.C. in 1941. There he joined Bill Farrimond, his friend and county colleague, who was captain and they guided the club to the first hat-trick of championship titles in the League's history. During the three seasons he was professional he claimed 243 wickets at a cheap rate and the club, after losing Hamer Cup finals in 1941 and 1942, managed to win the trophy against Heaton in 1943. To win four trophies from a possible eight is undoubtedly very impressive and the two famous Westhoughton cricketers had played a major part in bringing great pride and pleasure to their local club during troubled times.

Pollard played in four of the five 'Victory Tests' in 1945 and was the leading wicket-taker on either side. He was still not fully discharged from the Army in 1946 but bowled well for Lancashire when available and was selected for his maiden Test against India at Old Trafford. After reaching 124 without loss, India collapsed to 170 all out after Pollard turned the game around by claiming four wickets for seven runs in five overs. His outstanding performance of 5 for 24 in 27 overs is commemorated on the honours board in the Long Room at Old Trafford.

He was selected for the 1946/47 Ashes tour but did not possess enough pace to be successful and played in the one-off Test against New Zealand taking 3 for 73 in a rain-interrupted match. On his return to England he was impressive for Lancashire in 1947 taking 131 wickets including the best performance of his career, 8 for 33 against Northants at Old Trafford. It was not until 1948 however that he was selected for England again after Bradman's 'Invincibles' had easily won the first two Tests. At the age of 36 he opened the bowling with Alec Bedser at Old Trafford and took 3 for 53, including Bradman for 7, in 32 disciplined overs. Whilst batting he hit the close leg side fielder Sid Barnes under the ribs with a full-bloodied pull causing his removal on a stretcher and hospital observation for several days. In the same match there was another famous cricket injury as Denis Compton mishooked the ball onto his forehead and retired hurt before being stitched up and returning heroically to score 145 not out. Pollard was retained in the next Test at Headingley and again dismissed Bradman cheaply in the first innings but the little master had the last word in the

DICK POLLARD.

second innings as he completed his 29th and final century in Test cricket. Along with Arthur Morris, Bradman ensured Australia chased down 404 runs in the 344 minutes available to set a Test record for the highest score achieved in the fourth innings. It was Pollard's final Test but he had acquitted himself well taking 15 wickets at 25.20 in his four internationals.

In 1949 he was reasonably successful taking 73 wickets but Lancashire were beginning to rely more on young spin bowlers like Tattersall, Hilton and Berry. During the season he had a benefit which raised over £8,000, the third highest at the time, and was a true reflection of his popularity. During 1950 when Lancashire shared the Championship title with Surrey he played in five early fixtures but was then dropped as the spinners proved to be match-winners, and a young Brian Statham thankfully appeared on the scene. It is an interesting fact that Statham and Pollard only played one first-class match together when they opened the bowling against the West Indies tourists at Aigburth in July.

At the end of 1950 Pollard felt it was the right time to retire. He could be very proud that he had taken over 1,000 wickets for his native county and only nine bowlers have taken more. I have always felt that Pollard was similar in many respects to Ken Higgs. They were both big and strong, fully committed fast/medium swing and seam bowlers whose records for Lancashire were almost identical with Pollard taking 1,015 wickets at 22.15 and Higgs 1,033 at 22.90. They would certainly have made a wonderful opening pair had their careers coincided.

One cannot help but surmise that Pollard would have been closer to the 2,000 mark if he had not missed the war years when he would have been in his prime. He had played for England in four Tests and had won Championship medals in 1934 and 1950. He had thoroughly enjoyed his cricket career and returned to Westhoughton where he set up a business in cleaning materials but continued to play league cricket at weekends. He died in Westhoughton on 16th December 1985 at the age of 73.

Inns	Runs	HS	Ave	50/100	Balls	Runs	Wkts	BB	Ave	5w/10w	Ct
328	3522	63	13.29	7/0	62484	25314	1122	8-33	22.56	60/10	225

Alf Barlow

RHB/WK
b. 31st August 1915, Little Lever
d. 9th May 1983, Middleton
Career 1947-1951, 85 matches
Debut v Cambridge University, Old Trafford, 18th June 1947
HS: 44 v Derbyshire, Old Trafford 1949
BB: 0-0 v Warwickshire, Old Trafford 1950

ALFRED BARLOW was born at Little Lever, Bolton on 31st August 1915. He played cricket for his local club in the Bolton League before joining the Lancashire staff in 1947 at the age of 31. He was a reliable and unobtrusive wicketkeeper who had a great sense of humour and generally enjoyed life. He made his first-class debut at Old Trafford in 1947 against Cambridge University and *Wisden* on reviewing the season stated that: *'the new wicketkeeper Alf Barlow improved steadily and was a distinct acquisition.'*

Rather surprisingly he only played in five games in 1948 as Tom Brierley and Eric Edrich shared the wicketkeeping duties before they both retired at the end of the season. In 1949 Barlow and Alan Wilson, who joined the staff in 1948, were rivals for the position but in 1950 Barlow played in all 28 matches as Lancashire shared the Championship title with Surrey. It was Lancashire's best performance since 1934 and Barlow fully deserved to be awarded his county cap after keeping wicket so admirably.

During the winter of 1950-51 he was selected to tour India and Ceylon (now Sri Lanka) with the Commonwealth team which proved to be a long and exhausting experience. His county colleagues Ken Grieves and Jack Ikin were also included alongside some of the great players of the time like Ames, Laker, Worrell, Ramadhin, Tribe and Dooland. The team maintained an unbeaten record during a highly successful tour and gained the rubber in the unofficial Tests by winning two matches and drawing three. Barlow was not selected for any of the 'Tests' and suffered badly from insect bites, but nevertheless carried on enthusiastically and performed well in eleven of the other first-class games.

Alf Barlow, standing third from right, in the 1949 Lancashire team.

Sharing the County Championship title in 1950 and gaining selection for a Commonwealth tour proved to be the highlight of Barlow's five years at Lancashire as he only played in four Championship matches in 1951. Wilson was younger and an excellent wicketkeeper who became the preferred choice so Barlow, at the age of 35, decided his county career was over. He had played 74 matches for Lancashire, claiming 151 victims and scoring 707 runs at an average of 10.55. He continued to play league cricket for Middleton in the Central Lancashire League and in a 2005 poll was selected in the best Middleton team of the last 50 years by the cricketing public. He died at Middleton on 9th May 1983 at the age of 67.

Inns	Runs	HS	Ave	50/100	Balls	Runs	Wkts	BB	Ave	5w/10w	Ct/St
101	863	44	11.50	0/0	12	0	0	0-0	-	0/0	116/52

Roy Tattersall

LHB/OB
b. 17th August 1922, Tonge Moor
d. 9th December 2011, Kidderminster
Career 1948-1964, 328 matches
Debut v Glamorgan, Old Trafford, 19th May 1948
HS: 58 v Leicestershire, Old Trafford 1958
BB: 9-40 v Nottinghamshire, Old Trafford 1953
Tests: 16, 1950/51-1954
HS: 10* v India, Bombay 1951/52
BB: 7-52 v South Africa, Lord's 1951

ROY TATTERSALL was born in Tonge Moor, Bolton on 17th August 1922 and he played his early cricket at Bradshaw C.C. and Tonge C.C. in the Bolton League.

Initially he was a seam bowler and his success at league level led to him playing several games for the Lancashire Second Eleven in 1947. His debut for the first team followed against Glamorgan at Old Trafford the following year when he opened the bowling with Dick Pollard but failed to impress. He did, however, capture 66 wickets at 12.04 in the Second Eleven to play a major part in their Championship-winning season in the Minor Counties.

In 1949 Roy began to show great promise as an off spinner after taking the advice of Harry Makepeace to slow down and work on developing variations in flight, pace and length. He was also very fortunate to be tall with long fingers enabling him to impart the spin and bounce which troubles good batsmen. In 1950 he concentrated solely on bowling off spin for the first time, and what a summer he enjoyed taking 193 first-class wickets at an average of 13.59. He had played a major role in Lancashire finishing joint-winners of the County Championship with Surrey and furthermore

LANCASHIRE—JOINT CHAMPIONS, 1950

Standing (left to right) : R. Tattersall, M. Hilton, P. Greenwood, A. Barlow, R. Berry, K. Grieves.
Seated : G. A. Edrich, W. Place, N. D. Howard (captain), C. Washbrook, J. T. Ikin. Inset : B. Statham

he was the first winner of the Cricket Writers Club Young Cricketer of the Year trophy.

During such a golden summer it was somewhat surprising that Roy had been overlooked by the England selectors for the series against West Indies especially when seven spinners had been used. He did get his reward during the winter when, after injuries to Doug Wright and Trevor Bailey in Australia, he and his great friend Brian Statham were flown out to replace them. After taking four days to travel by air he made his Test debut against Australia at the Adelaide Oval where he claimed four wickets in a match that England lost. He was also selected for the final Test at Melbourne where he went wicketless but England beat Australia for the first time since 1938, although they lost the series 4-1. He was more successful in New Zealand taking 6 for 44 in Wellington as England won by six wickets with the other Test in the series drawn.

Several good judges felt that Roy was stale after his return from Australia early in 1951 but he nevertheless enjoyed a good series for England against the South African tourists. His best performance was at Lord's where he appears twice on the honours board in the same match with 7 for 52 and 5 for 49 in England's ten-wicket victory. At the end of the season the England party to tour India included not only Roy but also his fellow Lancastrians Nigel Howard (captain), Malcolm Hilton and Brian Statham. The series was drawn with one win each but the most interesting match was the fourth Test at Kanpur which England won by eight wickets. All four Lancastrians took the field with Howard as captain and, although Statham only bowled six overs in the match, Tattersall and Hilton enjoyed great success taking 17 of the twenty wickets to fall with Roy claiming 6 for 48 in the first innings. On a pitch tailor-made for spin the pair even opened the bowling in the second innings, a very rare occurrence for an England team.

In the return series in 1952 Jim Laker was the preferred choice of the England selectors and Roy only played two more Tests to end his disappointingly short international career with 58 wickets at 26.08 each in his 16 appearances. It seemed rather harsh especially when he had taken 8 for 28 and 5 for 48 in the first game of the season against Kent at Old Trafford, but Laker turned the ball more and proved to be the most skilful off spinner of his era. Despite his disappointment Roy continued to perform well for Lancashire and topped the bowling averages with 130 wickets at 17 runs each.

Another successful season followed in 1953 with 164 first-class victims, including 9 for 40 against Nottinghamshire at Old Trafford. Not only was this his best-ever performance but it also contained a hat-trick in a spectacular spell of seven wickets in 19 balls. In each of the following four seasons he continued to reach the hundred-wicket mark but in the late 1950's Cyril Washbrook, the captain, seemed to lose faith in him and he was often left out of the team with no reason given. Washbrook was rather aloof and lacked man-management skills, even dropping Roy and Malcolm Hilton into the second team when they had been awarded a joint benefit match in the Roses encounter at Old Trafford in 1960. Somewhat disenchanted with the latter part of his Lancashire career, Roy left the club at the end of the season having taken 1,369 first-class wickets at 18.03 each. Many of those victims were caught by the wonderful close catching trio of Jack Ikin, Ken Grieves and Geoff Edrich and Roy always gave them great credit for their skill and bravery. Lancashire had lost one of their best-ever spin bowlers and although he was 38 years old and his powers were declining his exit should have been more amicable and befitting for a popular, reserved and self-effacing gentleman.

Roy moved to Kidderminster where he played cricket for the local team in the Birmingham League and worked for a carpet firm. Just before he died in December 2011 at the age of 89, he considered it a great honour to have been invited to write the foreword in the official book celebrating Lancashire winning the Championship that summer. Authors Graham Hardcastle and Chris Ostick could not have made a better choice.

Inns	Runs	HS	Ave	50/100	Balls	Runs	Wkts	BB	Ave	5w/10w	Ct
369	2040	58	9.35	1/0	71132	24692	1369	9-40	18.03	99/18	146

Frank Tyson

RHB/RF
b. 6th June 1930, Farnworth
d. 27th September 2015, Queensland, Australia
Career 1952-1960, 244 matches
Debut: Northamptonshire v India, Northampton, 30th July 1952
HS: 82 v Sussex, Hove 1960
BB: 8-60 v Surrey, Kennington Oval 1957
Tests: 17, 1954-1958/59
HS: 37* v Australia, Brisbane 1954/55
BB: 7-27 v Australia, Melbourne 1954/55

FRANK TYSON, nicknamed 'Typhoon' Tyson after his demolition of Australia in the Ashes series of 1954/55, was born in Farnworth near Bolton on 6th June 1930. When he was very young his family moved to Middleton where Frank became obsessed with cricket despite his father and brother having no interest at all in the game. His cricket developed initially at Queen Elizabeth Grammar School, Middleton and at the age of fifteen he showed enough promise to be selected for Manchester Schools and also Middleton C.C. in the Central Lancashire League. He progressed well in senior cricket and helped Middleton win the Wood Cup in 1948 with his extreme pace. At eighteen he joined the Royal Signals at Catterick for compulsory National Service and continued to devote his next two summers to cricket, representing the Army at Lord's where he bowled Peter May for a duck.

Harry Makepeace, the Lancashire Coach, realised that Tyson had great potential and invited him to play for the county Second Eleven against Northumberland at Old Trafford in 1949. Unfortunately he arrived late and then pulled a muscle after bowling five overs and the following season he struggled to gain fitness after breaking a leg playing football. Lancashire lost faith in his durability and were unwilling to offer terms so he decided to follow a degree course at Durham University. Although Lancashire's lack of patience is understandable it is intriguing to imagine what might have happened if Tyson had signed a contract at Old Trafford in 1950, the same year as Brian Statham, when they were both aged twenty.

Thankfully Frank was undaunted by his injury problems and rejection by Lancashire. He struck lucky when Jock Livingston recommended him to Northants for a trial. He was offered a contract and made his maiden first-class appearance against India in 1952 at Northampton, dismissing Pankaj Roy by sheer pace in his first over. He had announced his arrival and fully intended to put the wind up batsmen wherever he played.

In the following season he continued to impress and *Wisden* suggested he might become a fine fast bowler after he dismissed some very good batsmen including Colin McDonald and Graeme Hole with the second and fourth balls of a fiery opening over against the Australian tourists. In 1954 he took 70 wickets at 20.92 and continued to embarrass and startle many batsmen with outright pace including Denis Compton and Bill Edrich. He was selected to play in the final Test against Pakistan at The Oval and made a good start opening the bowling with Brian Statham and taking 4 for 35. Tyson's arrival on the scene had alerted Len Hutton, the England captain, to his undoubted and rare potential and he was prepared to gamble on his pace and bounce being successful in Australia.

What followed in Australia has passed into the legend of the game. Tyson's achievement lay in creating, along with Brian Statham, one of the most effective fast bowling partnerships in the history of Ashes cricket. After a disastrous start in the first Test which Australia won by an innings and 154 runs, England won three of the next four Tests to retain the coveted trophy and the first rubber in Australia since the famous 'Bodyline' tour of 1932/33.

In the first Test Tyson had taken 1 for 160 in 29 overs but he decided to shorten his run-up in the state match against Victoria and captured six wickets by bowling at the same speed but with more accuracy. Hutton retained his faith in his strike bowler in the second Test at Sydney and, after being knocked unconscious by a Lindwall bouncer whilst batting, Tyson recovered to take 4 for 45 and 6 for 85 to gain a close victory by 38 runs. The tide had turned and he followed up with 7 for 27 in Melbourne as England won by 128 runs and yet another haul of 6 for 136 in the match as England were again victorious at Adelaide. Overall he ended the series with the outstanding figures of 28 wickets at the cost of 20.82 each. Australia had been humbled in a similar manner to the 'Bodyline' series with Tyson playing the role of Larwood although there was never any acrimony involved. There was a general opinion that nobody had ever bowled so fast as Tyson which was backed up by Don Bradman in the 1970s when he admitted he was the fastest he had ever seen. Len Hutton had taken a gamble which paid a handsome dividend and Tyson had become a heroic figure within the game of cricket. It was no surprise when he was chosen as one of *Wisden's* 'Five Cricketers of the Year' in the 1956 Almanack.

Against South Africa at Trent Bridge in the first Test of 1955 he continued where he had left off in Australia taking 6 for 28 in the second innings and in the third Test at Old Trafford he claimed a further six wickets, but he was never quite the same bowler again. In his final seven Tests he could manage only 14 wickets, and he was lucky to be chosen to tour Australia again in 1958/59 which was very much an anti-climax as England lost the series 4-0. Throughout his career he had suffered from injury and bowling at Northampton on a pitch that failed to offer pace and bounce. At Old Trafford or The Oval he may well have found conditions more to his liking and if he had played today he would have been cosseted by a central contract and treated as gold dust by captains and selectors as they search for express pace at international level. By 1960 Frank had decided to retire with an excellent record having taken 76 Test wickets at 18.56 and 767 first-class wickets at 20.92.

He became a teacher in Northampton for a short time but emigrated to Australia in 1962 where he continued in the teaching profession at Carey G.S. in Melbourne. In 1975 he became Coaching Director of Victoria and eventually Queensland, and he was also an accomplished journalist, author and broadcaster. Frank Tyson, like his equally famous predecessor Harold Larwood, died in Australia at the age of 85 on 27th September 2015 having enjoyed a very full and interesting life.

Inns	Runs	HS	Ave	50/100	Balls	Runs	Wkts	BB	Ave	5w/10w	Ct
316	4103	82	17.09	13/0	38173	16030	767	8-60	20.89	34/5	85

Jack Bond

RHB/LB
b. 6th May 1932, Kearsley
d. 11th July 2019, Bury
Career 1955-1974, 362 matches
List A 1963-1974, 99 matches
Debut v Surrey, Old Trafford, 3rd August 1955
HS: 157 v Hampshire, Old Trafford 1962
BB: 0-3 v Middlesex, Old Trafford 1965

JOHN DAVID BOND was born on 6th May 1932 in Kearsley, near Bolton but he soon moved to Little Hulton where his extended family lived very close together. He attended Hulton East Junior School where he was encouraged to play cricket by the headmaster before moving on to Bolton School where his ability as a tenacious batsman and excellent fielder was developed by the master in charge of cricket, Ron Booth, who played for Preston C.C. and Yorkshire's Second Eleven in his younger days.

Jack, as he was commonly known, had been a member at Walkden C.C. since his early teens and continued after leaving school in 1949 before serving two years' National Service from September 1950. He played for the station team and the Royal Army Pay Corps before returning to Walkden and the Bolton League in 1953. He enjoyed a good season averaging 43 and gained experience from watching and talking to the Walkden professional Edwin St. Hill, a former West Indian Test player. He was then persuaded to move to Radcliffe C.C. in 1954 to play in a better standard of cricket where he gained further valuable advice and encouragement from the Australian professional Cec Pepper. Eventually he was invited to winter coaching sessions at Old Trafford and was offered a contract for the 1955 season by Head Coach Stan Worthington.

Jack arrived at Old Trafford at a time of change as Winston Place, Jack Ikin and Geoff Edrich were all reaching the end of their careers and he found them all amicable and willing to pass on their experience. At the same time he became very friendly with Roy Tattersall, a fellow Boltonian, and they often travelled to matches together. Perhaps the person who influenced him most in his early days was Edrich, the kind and respected captain of the Second Eleven who became very much a father figure.

In his early years Jack was on the periphery of the first team and it was not until 1959 that he began to make his mark by scoring his first century against Nottinghamshire at Trent Bridge. Another average summer followed under the captaincy of Bob Barber before he experienced a fine summer in 1961 as a regular member of the team and was awarded his county cap after scoring 68 against Australia at Old Trafford. He felt that gaining his cap restored his self-belief and was an important factor in making 1962 his most successful season. New captain Joe Blackledge gave him a regular spot batting at number three and he responded with over two thousand runs, the last Lancashire player to achieve the feat. He was particularly proud to have recorded centuries against Yorkshire at both Old Trafford (109) and Headingley where he scored 144 and followed that in the next match with his highest first-class score of 157 against Hampshire at Old Trafford. The Roses match at Old Trafford that year was highly unusual in that all twenty-two players involved were born within their respective counties, and it must be doubtful if that will ever happen again.

After his outstanding season Jack was looking forward to 1963 with great confidence only to suffer a major setback when breaking his wrist facing Wes Hall in the West Indies tour match against Lancashire at Old Trafford. He never again regained the form he had displayed in the previous summer. From 1964 to 1967 he was in and out of the first team doing just enough to merit a contract, but one thing in his favour was that he impressed as captain of the Second Eleven and gained good results. It was nevertheless a bolt from the blue when he was appointed first team captain, initially on a temporary basis, for the 1968 season.

Lancashire had signed three cricketers who were to play vital roles in the future, particularly in one-day cricket which was becoming more and more popular. Clive Lloyd and Farokh Engineer were proven Test cricketers of quality whilst Jack Simmons, shrewdly plucked from league cricket at the age of 27, became one of the county's finest all-rounders. Jack had inherited the makings of a very good side and it was now his job to gain the respect of his fellow players and mould the team together. He firmly believed that his deep-rooted Methodist principles were a great help in his success as captain. He played cricket as he lived his life; he was honest, loyal, selfless and industrious, and he expected the same qualities from his team. In short his mantra was: 'team before self' and he stressed that if they enjoyed their cricket the crowd would too, and they would be successful as a result.

Lancashire celebrate the Gillette Cup and John Player League 'double' in 1970.

In 1969 Jack was excited by the introduction of the John Player League, a new 40-over per side competition played on Sunday afternoons. He immediately saw an opportunity to win a trophy. Most of the side had learned their cricket in the leagues and they adapted readily to the shorter format which required disciplined bowling, positive batting and enthusiastic fielding. During the next four years Jack would make his name as an exceptional captain and man manager who was universally popular with his fellow players and actually won trophies for his county. Lancashire were John Player League Champions in both 1969 and 1970, and won the Gillette Cup in three consecutive seasons from 1970 to 1972 with Jack himself providing one of the most memorable moments when his diving catch at extra cover, to dismiss Kent's Asif Iqbal, decisively turned the 1971 final Lancashire's way. He was rewarded by being chosen as one of *Wisden's* 'Five Cricketers of the Year' in 1971 and had transformed Lancashire into a confident and successful side in one-day cricket and improved their performances in the Championship. Following the third Lord's final he decided it was time to retire at the age of 40. His appointment as captain had been a master-stroke by the Committee. In his 18-year career he scored 11,867 runs including 14 centuries at an average of 26.60.

There followed a one-year period as joint coach at Old Trafford with John Savage before Jack moved to Nottinghamshire as Cricket Manager and captain and briefly serving as an England selector. Much better times were enjoyed however when he and his family moved to the Isle of Man for five years where he was employed as coach and groundsman at King William's College. He returned to Old Trafford as Manager for seven years up to 1986 when he left the club and soon became a first-class umpire, retiring in 1997. His love for Old Trafford continued however and he helped out at the ground into his eighties until he needed a hip replacement in 2015.

Jack died on 12th July 2019 at the age of 87 and his funeral was attended by many of his former team-mates, some of whom, including David Hughes from North America, had travelled great distances to show their respect and affection.

Jack Bond lived a full life and will be long remembered as one of Lancashire's best and most successful captains. He was respected not just for his captaincy but also his personal qualities and his sense of humour. He was indeed a proud Boltonian and a Lancashire lad through and through.

Inns	Runs	HS	Ave	50/100	Balls	Runs	Wkts	BB	Ave	5w/10w	Ct
548	12125	157	25.90	54/14	67	69	0	0-3	-	0/0	222

LIST A											
Inns	Runs	HS	Ave	50/100	Balls	Runs	Wkts	BB	Ave	4w/5w	Ct
74	698	43	12.92	0/0	-	-	-	-	-	-	31

Sir Neville Cardus and Jack Bond at Old Trafford.

John Roberts

RHB/RMF
b. 4th March 1933, Kearsley
d. 2nd December 2019, Bolton
Career 1957, 2 matches
Debut v Surrey, Old Trafford, 15th June 1957
HS: 5 v Cambridge University, Aigburth 1957
BB: 0-18 v Cambridge University, Aigburth 1957

JOHN FRANCIS ESDALE ROBERTS was born on 4th March 1933 at Kearsley near Bolton. He was tall and an ideal build for a fast bowler, initially playing for Kearsley C.C. in the Bolton League when Les Bulcock was professional. Early in his career he showed great promise as a tearaway paceman and was selected for Lancashire's Second Eleven in 1956 as the county searched for someone to partner Brian Statham. In 1957 his dream came true when he signed a one-year contract at Old Trafford and was given the opportunity to open the bowling with Statham in his debut match against Surrey. Sadly he was unable to impress against a formidable array of batsmen including three Test players in Mickey Stewart, Peter May and Ken Barrington who all passed fifty and Lancashire went on to lose the match by an innings and 51 runs. He was selected for the next fixture against Cambridge University at Aigburth where Lancashire were further embarrassed, losing once more by an innings with Bob Barber claiming seven Lancs wickets in the match. Unfortunately John was not re-engaged for the 1958 season as Ken Higgs was signed from Staffordshire. He returned to the leagues and eventually became a teacher.

As he matured and reduced in pace John became a very skilful seam and swing bowler who enjoyed a long and successful career as a professional in the Central Lancashire, Birmingham, Huddersfield and Ribblesdale leagues. The league he is most associated with, however, is the Bolton League where he played for Kearsley, Bradshaw and Tonge taking 671 wickets in total. In 1973 at the age of 40 he played as an amateur at Tonge winning the League bowling prize before he moved to Wigan C.C. in the Manchester Association near the end of his career.

John was not only a talented bowler but also a fully qualified and accomplished coach who provided expert advice to many youngsters over the years. He was also instrumental in recommending Haseeb Hameed at the age of eight for a trial with the Lancashire schools Primary team after

John Roberts claims the wicket of fellow Boltonian and ex-Lancs and England cricketer Charlie Hallows for Kearsley against Astley Bridge.

being impressed by his ability as he practised in the nets at Tonge C.C. He regularly ran courses aimed at developing coaches to pass on their knowledge to aspiring cricketers and players of the calibre of Cec Wright and Annesley de Silva attended and very much appreciated one such course in 1980 at the Withington Indoor school.

John was held in such high regard in the Bolton League that he was made a Life Member in 2003 and received a Lifetime Achievement Award in 2009 for the decades of cricket coaching he had delivered to develop and inspire thousands of young players. He was a prime example of someone who put back far more into the game than he ever took from it. He will long be remembered, particularly in the Bolton area, for his enthusiastic and competitive approach to the game and his outstanding skills as a bowler, coach and administrator.

Inns	Runs	HS	Ave	50/100	Balls	Runs	Wkts	BB	Ave	5w/10w	Ct
4	5	5	2.50	0/0	156	90	0	0-18	-	0/0	0

Duncan Worsley

LHB/OB
b. 18th July 1941, Farnworth
Career 1960-1967, 113 matches
List A 1964-1967, 3 matches
Debut v South Africa, Blackpool, 3rd September 1960
HS: 139 v Oxford University v Middlesex, The Parks 1961
BB: 4-21 v Leicestershire, Grace Road 1966

DUNCAN ROBERT WORSLEY was born in Townley's Hospital, Farnworth, Bolton on 18th July 1941. He attended St. Simon & Jude School, Great Lever, before moving to Bolton School in 1949 where his love of cricket was fostered. He lived on Green Lane and became a member of Bolton C.C. at a very young age but after promising performances for the Bolton School under 14 team decided to join Farnworth C.C. He profited from good early coaching from Charlie Hallows, Ron Booth at Bolton School and Jim Gledhill at Farnworth who was in the process of developing his youth policy which eventually brought great success to the club.

Duncan made his debut for the first team at the age of 14 in 1955 but did not appear regularly until 1958 when he began to play a more significant role, especially in 1959 when Farnworth won the League title. Up to the age of 19 his career at club level ran parallel to that at Bolton School who had a competitive fixture list against strong opposition such as Lancashire Club & Ground, MCC, Manchester Grammar School, Bradford Grammar School and Lancaster Royal Grammar School as well as a southern tour involving strong opponents at school and club level. He must certainly look back on 1960 as one of the most enjoyable years of his life and few schoolboys can have experienced such a successful end to their school careers.

In early January he was a member of the school team that won the Public Schools six-a-side football competition but it was in cricket that he really excelled. He captained the school team which was unbeaten in 21 games and which Ron Booth stated was probably the best he had coached in his long career. He was top scorer for the unbeaten Lancashire Cricket Federation under 19's team including centuries against Lincolnshire at Burghley Park and Cambridgeshire at Fenners. He played twelve games for Lancashire's Second Eleven with a top score of 132 against Northumberland. He was a member of the Farnworth C.C. team that won the League and Cup 'double' with Alan Rushton as captain and Frank Hodgkiss as professional. The

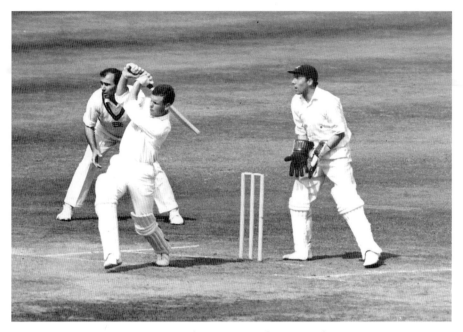

Duncan Worsley in action for Lancashire.

crowning glory, however, was his selection for the Lancashire First Eleven to make his first-class debut against the South African tourists at Stanley Park, Blackpool in September. He opened the batting with Alan Wharton who was playing his final match before moving to Leicestershire and although he only made 6 in the first innings he batted solidly to reach 28 in the second prompting *Wisden* to state: "Worsley of Bolton School showed much promise." Added to all this success in the cricket world Duncan could also rejoice at the news he had been offered a place to study History at St. Edmund Hall, Oxford University in October. It was the icing on the cake and would enable him to develop both academically and as a cricketer.

In 1961 Oxford University cricket was overshadowed by the serious car accident involving the Oxford captain, the Nawab of Pataudi who lost an eye. Pataudi was an outstanding and unorthodox batsman aged 20 who, up to the time of the injury, had scored 1,216 runs with an average of 55.27 including four centuries, and it was generally agreed he would become one of the great Test players. Despite his serious handicap he went on to play 46 Tests for India, 40 as captain, and scored six centuries with an average of 34.91. One can only imagine what he may have achieved without his impairment.

Oxford were a good side in 1961 and included not only Pataudi but players of the calibre of Abbas Ali Baig, David Green, David Pithey and Colin Dryborough so Duncan needed to perform well to earn his blue. He did not impress in his first three county matches, but against Middlesex and the bowling of Test players Alan Moss and Fred Titmus he scored his maiden first-class century finishing with 139 in a big partnership with Pataudi. Soon afterwards another very good innings of 80 against the Australian tourists at The Parks ensured he was cementing his place in the side and by the end of the season he had registered 754 runs for Oxford at 24.32 and won the first of his four Blues.

In 1962 Oxford experienced an unhappy season but Duncan reached his second first-class century against the Free Foresters and batted well to score 67 and 60 against Lancashire at The Parks. He was often the only Blue available because of exams and he captained the side regularly and performed with great credit in scoring 772 runs at 27.57 in difficult circumstances. In the following summer Pataudi returned as captain and Duncan was appointed vice-captain playing only 8 games in his final exam year and scoring 344 runs at 22.93.

In 1964 he captained the Oxford team after staying on for a fourth year to study for a teaching diploma. He enjoyed a good season scoring 684 runs at 32.57 but team results were disappointing as his bowlers were unable to support the batsmen and his best players were often unavailable taking exams or were injured. In the second half of the summer he made an impressive contribution to the Lancashire batting and was welcomed back into the fold. It was his best season in first-class cricket with 1,498 runs at 31.87 including 104 against Kent at Blackpool and 100 versus Sussex at Eastbourne.

1965 proved to be a lean season for Duncan but he bounced back in 1966 finishing second in the batting averages to Geoff Pullar and was awarded his county cap. He appeared in 13 County matches in 1967 but after careful consideration decided to retire and further his career in education. He had shared his first-class career almost equally between Oxford University and Lancashire and left with a decent record having scored 5,062 runs at 26.09 including four centuries, and taken 37 wickets at 41.08.

On retiring Duncan was immediately offered a professional contract by Farnworth C.C., his former club in the Bolton League where he had started as a youngster. Although he had always been regarded as a quality batsman there were questions about how he would fare as an off-spinner but they were soon answered. Duncan was tall with long fingers and he worked hard to really spin the ball and control line and length. After a quiet start in his first year, he was so successful in 1969 and 1970 that he won the Professional Prize in both years and his club won the Hamer Cup in 1969. He won the Professional Prize again in 1974 when he scored two centuries against Little

Lever and took all 10 wickets against Bradshaw, but after a dispute with the club he left before the start of the 1976 season, deciding to play as an amateur at Worsley C.C. in the Manchester Association.

During the magnificent summer of 1976 Worsley were a good side but the club had not won the league title since 1932. The news that Duncan was joining in early April lifted the players to new heights and he made a massive difference. He thoroughly enjoyed his season "without pressure" topping the league averages with 882 runs at 58.71 and taking 49 wickets at 13.22. The title was duly secured and the club could finally celebrate.

In 1977 he returned to the Bolton League as professional at Bradshaw C.C. and was immediately successful winning the League title and Hamer Cup as well as the Professional Prize for the fourth time. The only other two players to have won the prize on four occasions were Les Bulcock and Fred Hartley, two of the best players to grace the Bolton League. Duncan stepped down as professional at the end of 1979 but continued at the club for two years, winning the Amateur Player of the Year award in 1981. From 1982 to 1984 he moved to Heaton C.C. as professional and at the time of his retirement had scored 10,123 runs and taken 1,137 wickets. It was an exceptional achievement and he was the first player to complete the double of 10,000 runs and 1,000 wickets which has since been achieved by another fine player David White.

Duncan Worsley is without doubt a true legend of Bolton League cricket.

Inns	Runs	HS	Ave	50/100	Balls	Runs	Wkts	BB	Ave	5w/10w	Ct
205	5062	139	26.09	25/4	3422	1520	37	4-21	41.08	0/0	68

LIST A											
Inns	Runs	HS	Ave	50/100	Balls	Runs	Wkts	BB	Ave	4w/5w	Ct
3	77	39	25.66	0/0	-	-	-	-	-	-	1

Kevan Tebay

RHB
b. 2nd February 1936, Bolton
d. 13th August 1996, Bolton
Career 1961-1963, 15 matches
Debut v Gloucestershire, Cheltenham, 16th August 1961
HS: 106 v Hampshire, Old Trafford 1962
Did not bowl

KEVAN TEBAY was born in Bolton on 2nd February 1936. He was a pupil at Thornleigh College when he started playing cricket at Tonge C.C. where he won the League under 18 batting prize in 1952 aged 16. He impressed the club selectors by making two centuries in his aggregate of 439 runs and was quickly promoted to the first team. A few years later he moved to Astley Bridge C.C. and continued to show his class which resulted in him being selected for Lancashire's Second Eleven. He played regularly during 1959 and 1960 and was offered a county contract halfway through the 1960 season.

He made his debut for Lancashire's first team against Gloucestershire in 1961 in partnership with Edward Craig, a nineteen years-old student who had scored over one thousand runs that summer opening the batting with Mike Brearley at Cambridge University. The highlight of Kevan's fifteen-match career at Lancashire, however, was the 106 he scored against Hampshire at Old Trafford in 1962 after coming to the wicket with the score standing at 14 for 4 and two Test bowlers, Derek Shackleton and Butch White, asking searching questions. Later in the season he played in the Roses Match at Old Trafford which was highly unusual for the fact that every member of the Lancashire team was born in the red rose county, and every member of the Yorkshire side was born in the white rose county. Typically rain was the eventual winner as the match was drawn but the special circumstances were certainly memorable and unlikely to be repeated.

In 1963 Kevan opened the batting with Brian Booth against Worcestershire at Old Trafford and they shared partnerships of 170 in the first innings and 103 in the second which, at the time, was only the seventh occasion it had been achieved for Lancashire. Another interesting statistic surrounding the match was that Jack Flavell completed a hat-trick with lbw decisions, only the second time this had happened in first-class cricket. Even though Kevan had scored 97 and 60 in the game he was not re-engaged for the 1964 season and ended his first-class career having scored 509 runs at 20.36.

On returning to the Bolton League he joined Astley Bridge C.C. in 1964 and Egerton C.C. two years later where he won successive Hamer Cup medals in 1970 and 1971 before a two-year spell at Little Lever C.C. brought a League and Cup 'double' in 1972. He finally returned to Egerton, the club with which he is mostly associated, and retired in 1978 having scored 6,596 runs. He had three sons who all played in the Bolton League with Paul being an outstanding batsman scoring over 10,000 runs and winning the League batting prize on two occasions.

Kevan will long be remembered in the Bolton area for the quality of his batting and the fact that he was a strong character. He died on 13th August 1996 at the age of 60.

Inns	Runs	HS	Ave	50/100	Balls	Runs	Wkts	BB	Ave	5w/10w	Ct
27	509	106	20.36	2/1	-	-	-	-	-	-	3

Brian Krikken

LHB/WK
b. 26th August 1946, Horwich
Career 1966-1969, 3 matches
Debut v Oxford University, The Parks, 8th June 1966
HS: 4 v Oxford University, The Parks 1966
and 4 Worcestershire v Cambridge University, Halesowen 1969
Did not bowl

BRIAN EGBERT KRIKKEN was born in Horwich on 26th August 1946. He was an outstanding wicketkeeper who played most of his cricket with Westhoughton and Horwich but also represented Eagley and Tonge. His father had kept wicket for Horwich and Eagley and his son Karl played for Astley Bridge before enjoying a very successful first-class career as gloveman at Derbyshire C.C.C. In his book on the Bolton League, Arthur Hargreaves stated that Brian made, "the heavens ring with his almost continuous and loud appealing" and it is no coincidence that Karl was renowned as the noisiest 'keeper on the county circuit.

Derek Hamblett (left) and Brian Krikken opening the batting for Westhoughton against Horwich at The Recreation Ground in the 1960s.

Brian attended Rivington & Blackrod Grammar School and in 1962 was selected for the Lancashire Federation under 19's team when he was barely 16. He impressed the selectors and remained in the squad for the following three years playing alongside three future county stalwarts; David Lloyd, David Hughes and Frank Hayes. In 1965, his final year, there were actually seven boys from the Bolton League in a very strong Federation side which may well have created a record. Apart from Brian the other six were: Derek Holdsworth, David Hughes, Roger Sutcliffe, Les McKnight, Mike Hardcastle and Keith Eccleshare. Another unusual occurrence was the fact that four boys from Bolton School were selected during the season, namely Derek and Roger above plus Chris Williams and Ian Nuttall.

During 1965 Brian had made his debut for Lancashire's Second Eleven and he was offered a contract for the 1966 and 1967 seasons. He played regularly for the seconds where he was nicknamed 'Doctor' which alluded to the infamous Crippen and was typical of dressing room humour. In June 1966, at the age of 19, he made his debut in the same match as Alan Thomas against Oxford University at The Parks taking three catches and scoring 4 and 0. The following year he played his second and final first-class game for Lancashire against Scotland at Old Trafford claiming two further catches and scoring four with the bat. It is an interesting fact that Brian's five catches in his two Lancashire appearances were all off the bowling of Peter Lever. He was to take part in one other first-class match for Worcestershire against Cambridge University at Halesowen in 1969 where he did not bat but made two more catches.

After his brief involvement in county cricket Brian returned to the Bolton League, winning the league wicketkeeping prize in 1975 when at Westhoughton, and on retiring he had claimed 422 dismissals. More recently he has been named as wicketkeeper in the best-ever team to have represented Tonge and also Westhoughton, and it is generally agreed that he is one of the most skilful 'keepers to have played in the Bolton League.

Inns	Runs	HS	Ave	50/100	Balls	Runs	Wkts	BB	Ave	5w/10w	Ct/St
3	8	4	2.66	0/0	-	-	-	-	-	-	7/0

Alan Thomas

RHB/OB
b. 7th January 1947, Bolton
Career 1966, 1 match
Debut v Oxford University, The Parks, 8th June 1966
HS: 4 v Oxford University, The Parks 1966
BB: 0-7 v Oxford University, The Parks 1966

ALAN THOMAS was born in Bolton on the 7th January 1947 and was something of a prodigy when he arrived on the cricket scene in the early 1960's. He attended Canon Slade Grammar School where he played for the first eleven as a twelve year old before being selected for the Bolton under 15's team in the Lancashire Schools Cricket Association competition. From there he advanced to the County under 15 team joining such talented players as David Lloyd and Frank Hayes who both progressed to captain Lancashire and play for England.

At club level he was originally a junior member at Heaton CC representing the third team at the age of 13 but after attending nets at the Clarendon Street Indoor School run by Jim Gledhill and Billy Greenhalgh was encouraged to move to Farnworth C.C. where he was in the first team at the age of 14. Word of his precocious talent spread quickly and after playing for the Lancashire Federation under 19 team in 1963 he was picked for Lancashire's Second Eleven against Cumberland scoring 8 not out and 17 not out. As a matter of interest the Lancashire Federation in 1963 and 1964 when Alan played enjoyed great success winning 11 matches and and losing only one with a very strong set of players that included David Lloyd, Frank Hayes, David Hughes, Brian Krikken, Bill Taylor, Martin Greenhalgh, Bob Green and Roger Sutcliffe.

In 1964 Alan continued to progress with good performances for Farnworth and the Lancashire Federation and at the age of 18 Lancashire offered him a place on the staff for the 1965 season. Playing Second Eleven and Minor Counties cricket he scored nearly 500 runs with an average of 26 and took 14 wickets but in 1966 it appeared that he was being treated more as an off-spinner who could bat in the middle order rather than a front line batsman as he recorded only 152 runs with the bat whilst bowling 276 overs for 26 wickets. It was not really what Alan had expected yet he was delighted to make what turned out to be his only first-class appearance against Oxford University at The Parks, scoring 4 & 0 batting at number eight, and taking 0 for 7 in 8 overs. It was somewhat ironic that at the end of the season he won the batting prize in the Bolton League with 489 runs at 48.90. He left Old Trafford for more security in an office job and joined Farnworth Social Circle as professional in 1967 at the age of 20.

Farnworth Social Circle C.C. had evaded the honours board since 1925 but Alan proved to be a great acquisition inspiring the side to win the Cross Cup in his first season. In 1969 they won the League title and such was his influence in his 11 years at the club that 3 League titles and 4 Cross Cups were won including a League and Cup 'double' in 1972. His league record of 1,073 runs in a season in 1972 was beaten by Mudassar Nazar, the Pakistan Test player, in 1976 and it was a strange quirk of fate that Alan was bowling at the time.

In 1978 he felt like a change of club and moved to Clifton C.C. for three years and then Horwich C.C. in 1981 and 1982 before returning to Clifton until he retired in 1987 aged 40. In his career in the Bolton Association he had set an aggregate record with over 11,000 runs and taken more than 500 wickets. Alan had proved to be a local legend and can feel very proud of his outstanding achievements.

Inns	Runs	HS	Ave	50/100	Balls	Runs	Wkts	BB	Ave	5w/10w	Ct
2	4	4	2.00	0/0	48	7	0	0-7	-	0/0	0

Mike Watkinson

RHB/OB, RM
b. 1st August 1961, Westhoughton
Career 1982-1999, 308 matches
List A 1982-2000, 376 matches
Debut v Kent, Old Trafford, 28th August 1982
HS: 161 v Essex, Old Trafford 1995
BB: 8-30 v Hampshire, Old Trafford 1994
Tests: 4 1995-1995/96
HS: 82* v West Indies, Trent Bridge 1995
BB: 3-64 v West Indies, Old Trafford 1995
ODI: 1 match 1995/96
Did not bat
BB: 0-43 v South Africa, Johannesburg 1995/96

MICHAEL WATKINSON was born in Westhoughton on 1st August 1961 and was a pupil at Westhoughton County Primary School when he first became interested in cricket. He joined Westhoughton C.C. at a very young age and represented the under 18s team aged eleven and was a member of the first team by the age of fifteen. At Rivington & Blackrod High School he was selected to represent the Bolton under 15s team and later played for the Lancashire Schools Cricket Association under 19s team and the Lancashire Federation. Throughout this period he learned a great deal from coaches Teddy Gerrard, Frank  Holbrook and Derek Heaton, and he developed so well that he was offered professional terms at British Aerospace C.C. in 1980 at the age of 18.

By scoring 1,390 runs at 37.56 and taking 190 wickets at 12.17 in his two seasons as professional Mike proved that he was a quality all-rounder and was awarded the professional prize in 1981 aged 20. Lancashire C.C.C. and Manager Jack Bond in particular were aware of Watkinson's potential and after playing 14 matches for Cheshire in 1982 he made his county debut in the same match as Neil Fairbrother against Kent at Old Trafford. He was offered a professional contract for the following season and settled in quickly playing 15 games with two six-wicket returns against Sussex and Glamorgan. His county career had started in earnest and over the next

sixteen years he would prove to be one of Lancashire's best-ever all-rounders.

Tall, good looking, intelligent, immaculate in appearance and possessing a dry sense of humour, Mike was initially a medium pace swing and seam bowler who later became an off-spinner. He was an attacking middle order batsman good enough to score over 1,000 runs with an average of nearly 40 in 1993 and was used as a 'pinch-hitter' when opening in one-day cricket. Interestingly he was nicknamed 'Winker' after his name was misprinted on a scorecard as Watkins who was a character in the Dandy comic named 'Winker Watkins'.

In 1984 Mike won the first of 10 medals as a Lancashire player when Warwickshire were beaten in the B&H Cup final at Lord's whilst the following season he hit the first of his 11 centuries in the game against Surrey at Southport. After the end of season disappointment at losing to Sussex in the 1986 NatWest Trophy final big changes were made at Old Trafford ahead of the 1987 season. The manager Jack Bond and coach Peter Lever were dismissed; Clive Lloyd was replaced as captain by David Hughes and Alan Ormrod was appointed Manager with John Savage as Coach. At the beginning of February the Chairman of 18 years, Cedric Rhoades, was forced to resign by intense pressure from an action group and the Committee moved swiftly by inviting Bob Bennett to take over. Immediately there was a marked improvement in attitude and performance by the players which gave members and supporters much hope for the future and the new captain, manager and chairman could take a great deal of credit for Lancashire finishing second in the County Championship. In actual fact they would have won the title if they had been able to dismiss the last pair in the Yorkshire match at Old Trafford when they held out for 17.5 overs to draw the game. On another occasion the match against Derbyshire was thrown away when, after needing 5 runs to win with 3 wickets left, Lancashire lost by 3 runs. In the end Nottinghamshire were champions by just 4 points. Although disappointed by the end result Lancashire followers were greatly enthused by the new spirit within the club and the very talented group of young players that were beginning to emerge. The stage had been set for better times ahead and Mike would play an important part.

In 1988 Lancashire beat a strong Worcestershire team in the final of the inaugural Refuge Assurance Cup competition at Edgbaston and Mike was named Man of the Match after scoring an unbeaten 42 and bowling the dangerous Graeme Hick. The good run continued in 1989 as Lancashire won the One-Day League and in 1990 became the first team to do the 'cup double' winning both Lord's finals with Mike again Man of the Match in the B&H Cup win against Worcestershire and at the crease when the NatWest Trophy was secured with victory over Northants.

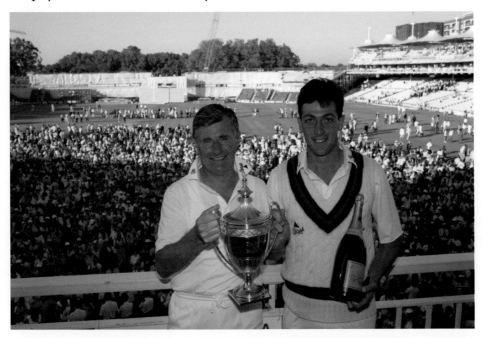

Mike Watkinson with skipper David Hughes after winning the Man of the Match award in the 1990 Benson and Hedges Cup final.

Mike captained Lancashire from 1994 to 1997 and in his first year achieved the best bowling performance of his career when he captured 8 for 30 against Hampshire at Old Trafford. It was a remarkable coincidence that only three weeks earlier Wasim Akram had recorded exactly the same figures against Somerset at Southport, and both were the best performances since Roy Tattersall's 9 for 40 against Nottinghamshire at Old Trafford in 1953. In scoring 117 in the same match Mike could also be very proud to become only the third Lancashire player after Johnny Briggs and Len Hopwood to score a century and take ten wickets in the same match. A fourth place finish in the Championship was the best result of his captaincy but there was further one-day success in the 1995 B&H Cup and another 'cup double' in 1996 with the B&H Cup retained alongside the NatWest Trophy.

When Mike played in his first Test against West Indies at Old Trafford in 1995 he became the fourth player from Westhoughton C.C. to have represented England after Dick Tyldesley, Bill Farrimond and Dick Pollard. He acquitted himself well scoring 37 and taking 2 for 28 and 3 for 64 but it was Dominic Cork who stole the limelight as he took a hat-trick in the opening over of the fourth day, the first one for England since Peter Loader, also against West Indies, at Leeds in 1957. In the next Test at Trent Bridge Mike scored 82 not out and took 3 for 84 but had a quiet match in the following Test at the Oval playing alongside fellow Lancastrians Michael Atherton, John Crawley and Jason Gallian. He was selected to tour South Africa in the winter of 1995/96 and played in one Test and one One-Day International finishing his Test career with 167 runs at 33.40 and 10 wickets at 34.80.

His final years at Old Trafford included yet another one-day 'double' in 1998 with the One-Day League title and victory over Derbyshire in the NatWest Final at Lord's, and the One-Day League title was retained in 1999. Mike retired from first-class cricket at the end of 1999 with an outstanding career record of 10,683 runs at 26.84 and 720 wickets at 33.64 whilst in one-day cricket he was equally impressive with 5,317 runs and his 373 wickets are the second highest total behind Jack Simmons. He was a very proud and dedicated Lancastrian and the fact that his Benefit Year in 1996 raised £209,000 reflected his popularity.

After retiring as a player he became Second Eleven Coach for two years before following Bob Simpson as Cricket Manager in 2002. A highly-qualified Level 4 coach, Mike was very involved in advising Andrew Flintoff and James Anderson in particular in the early part of their careers. His expertise was recognised by England when he was invited to work with Duncan Fletcher as bowling coach on tours to Bangladesh and Sri Lanka.

In 2007 Lancashire once more found themselves in touching distance of the Championship title when they bravely chased a total of 489 in the final match against Surrey. The fact that they reached 464 was a county record for a fourth innings total but nevertheless it was another glorious failure and the search for the greatest domestic prize continued.

In 2011 under a new structure with Mike as Director of Cricket and Peter Moores as Head Coach Lancashire, with a team of mostly home-grown players, finally hit the jackpot as they claimed the Championship outright for the first time since 1934. At the start of the season many felt the team would struggle to stay in the first division but through sheer determination, team spirit and a 'backs to the wall' attitude the players managed to turn around matches that appeared to be lost. Even on the last day of the season leaders Warwickshire were strong favourites but Hampshire held on to draw their game as Lancashire defeated Somerset by eight wickets to spark great scenes of celebration at Taunton and by Lancastrians at home and indeed, around the world. Finally there was a great feeling of relief and elation among Lancashire cricket lovers.

Mike left the club at the end of the 2014 season after 32 years' service as an outstanding all-rounder, a successful captain, a quality coach and skilled administrator. Latterly he played some league cricket in the Bolton area for Egerton and Edgworth alongside his son Liam who is talented enough to have represented Leeds/Bradford University in four first-class matches as well as Cumberland in the Minor Counties Competition. In 2015 Mike was appointed Master in charge of Cricket at Manchester Grammar School and promoted to Director of Sport in 2019. He is very happy in his new role and relishing the challenge ahead.

Inns	Runs	HS	Ave	50/100	Balls	Runs	Wkts	BB	Ave	5w/10w	Ct
459	10939	161	26.68	50/11	47809	24960	739	8-30	33.77	27/3	156

LIST A											
Inns	Runs	HS	Ave	50/100	Balls	Runs	Wkts	BB	Ave	4w/5w	Ct
296	5398	130	22.97	20/2	16057	12152	381	5-44	31.89	7/3	98

Karl Krikken

RHB/WK
b. 9th April 1969, Bolton
Career 1988/89-2003, 214 matches
List A 1987-2003, 203 matches
T20 2003, 1 match
Debut: Griqualand West v Eastern Province B, Kimberley, 3rd February 1989
HS: 104 Derbyshire v Lancashire, Old Trafford 1996
BB: 1-54 Derbyshire v Hampshire, Derby 1999

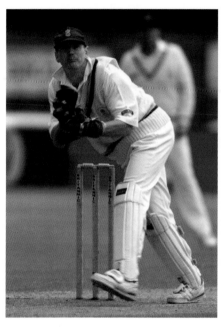

KARL KRIKKEN was born into a cricketing family who specialised in keeping wicket in the Bolton League. His grandfather Hilbert played for Horwich and Eagley whilst his father Brian was good enough to 'keep in two first-class matches for Lancashire and one for Worcestershire. Karl, however, was the most talented with superb hands, nimble feet and quick reactions who was particularly good standing up to the wicket. He had worshipped Alan Knott and Bob Taylor as a budding gloveman and although he possessed similar skills he had nothing of their style. 'Krikk' lived on his nerves and was labelled the noisiest and most fidgety 'keeper on the county circuit.

Karl, whose ancestors came from the Netherlands, was born in Bolton on 9th April 1969 and attended Rivington & Blackrod High School. As a youngster he played for Horwich, Tonge and British Aerospace before moving to Astley Bridge. In 1982 he was selected for the Lancashire Schools under 13 team and manager Martin Wadsworth's seasonal report stated: "Karl Krikken has kept wicket in all matches and is truly accomplished whether standing up or standing back." He progressed to the Lancashire Schools under 15 team gaining his cap in 1984 whilst at League level he was awarded the Bolton League wicketkeeping prize in 1985, 1986 and 1987 playing for Astley Bridge.

Karl had been keen to play professional cricket for his native Lancashire initially but Warren Hegg had already displayed his all-round talents at Old Trafford as an 18 year-old so he decided to look elsewhere. After his selection for the England Schools team his father approached Derbyshire for a trial and Karl made his Second Eleven debut in 1986 aged 17. He had to wait a couple of years before receiving a contract but in 1989 he was selected for the first team as a middle order batsman in the first instance and later in the season against Leicestershire caught three and stumped one when he was given the opportunity to keep wicket.

Karl Krikken signs his first contract for Derbyshire.

Karl replaced Bernie Maher as Derbyshire's regular 'keeper in 1990 and held the position until the end of 2002, gaining his county cap in 1992. In his first summer he claimed 63 victims but his most successful year was 1996 with 67 dismissals and 882 runs at 40.09 including his maiden century at Old Trafford. He was an unorthodox batsman who was difficult to dislodge and had the ability to drive opponents to distraction. He scored over 500 runs in a season on three occasions and although he made only one century, he hit 93 not out against Nottinghamshire in 2001. In the 1993 Benson & Hedges Cup final at Lord's he produced one of his best innings in a 77-run partnership with Dominic Cork which ensured a challenging target was set, one that Lancashire were unable to reach.

His first-class batting record of 5,725 runs at 21.76 was sound rather than eye-catching but he played in an age when wicketkeepers were valued more for their glove work than their ability to score heavily. Only four Derbyshire wicketkeepers have exceeded his total of 557 victims and none have bettered his average of 2.6 victims per match. He very much resented giving byes away and on five occasions kept a 'clean sheet' in totals over 400, whilst against Hampshire at Chesterfield in 1997 he did not concede a bye in a match total of 732 runs. He was without doubt a quality wicketkeeper, a doughty competitor and great team man who was well respected on the county scene.

On retiring in 2003 he was appointed Second Eleven Coach and subsequently became Director of the Derbyshire Academy. In 2011 he followed John Morris as Head Coach and in 2014 became Director of Cricket at Shropshire, winning the ECB National Cricket Coach of the Year award as well. In 2018 he joined Lancashire taking on the role of Lead Coach at the Indoor Cricket Centre and also coaching the Lancashire under 14 team. Early in 2019 he was appointed Performance Manager with responsibility for Lancashire's under 10-under 13 squads and works closely with Performance Director Mark Chilton, Academy Director Gary Yates and under 14s-under 17s age group Performance Manager Stephen Titchard. All four coaches are former Lancashire age group players and talented county cricketers who know and fully understand the Lancashire pathway to county cricket. Young aspiring Lancashire players are in good hands.

Inns	Runs	HS	Ave	50/100	Balls	Runs	Wkts	BB	Ave	5w/10w	Ct/St
323	5725	104	21.76	25/1	134	121	1	1-54	121.00	0/0	526/31

LIST A											
Inns	Runs	HS	Ave	50/100	Balls	Runs	Wkts	BB	Ave	4w/5w	Ct/St
138	1671	55	18.77	1/0	-	-	-	-	-	-	196/44

T20											
Inns	Runs	HS	Ave	50/100	Balls	Runs	Wkts	BB	Ave	4w/5w	Ct/St
1	3	3*	-	0/0	-	-	-	-	-	-	1/0

Jason Kerr

RHB/RMF
b. 7th April 1974, Bolton
Career 1993-2002, 65 matches
List A 1993-2002, 113 matches
Debut: Somerset v Australia, Taunton, 8th May 1993
HS: 80 Somerset v West Indies, Taunton 1995
BB: 7-23 Somerset v Leicestershire, Taunton 1999

JASON IAN DOUGLAS KERR was born in Bolton on 7th April 1974. His father Lenny played cricket for Tonge C.C. and it was here that Jason learned the skills of the game and how to compete in youth matches. He has a younger brother Andrew who also developed into a top quality batsman at Tonge C.C. and Greenmount C.C. and was good enough to play for Derbyshire's Second Eleven.

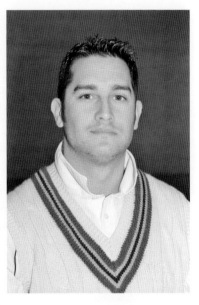

In 1987 Jason impressed the selectors and was picked for the Lancashire Schools under 13 team in a very strong squad that included Glen Chapple and they both made significant contributions to a successful season in which six matches were won and four drawn. The following year he was in the Lancashire under 14 team that won the NatWest Trophy at Taunton School and in 1989 enjoyed both individual and team success in a Lancashire under 15 side that was very difficult to beat.

Jason had proved to be an important member of the Lancashire Schools cricket teams for the past three years but he had never experienced a year like 1990. He was maturing quickly as a right hand batsman and right arm fast/medium bowler and began to make his presence felt at Tonge. He won a Hamer Cup medal at the age of 16 as Greenmount were beaten in the final and was also awarded the Bolton League 'Under 16 Player of the Year' trophy. Furthermore he played for the formidable Lancashire under 16 team that won the national Texaco County Championship title in the finals at Uppingham School, a feat last achieved in the days of Michael Atherton and Warren Hegg in 1984. The team produced a staggering 100% record, winning all 13 games during the season, and Kerr scored five fifties in his 10 innings. In browsing through an old scorebook I found it interesting that he opened the batting against the North of England under 15 team at Burnley C.C. and was bowled by Michael Vaughan but not before he had registered a classy 58. It was very clear that there were boys in the Lancashire under 16 team who were capable of playing at a higher level and, after attending trials at Somerset in 1992, both Jason and Andrew Payne from Rawtenstall were offered contracts. In the winter they were both selected for the England under 19 tour to India in early 1993 along with their former Lancashire team-mates Glen Chapple and Peter Wilcock.

On his return Jason made his debut for Somerset aged 19 against the Australian tourists at Taunton scoring 12 in his only innings. He fared better with the ball taking three wickets, including the prolific David Boon as his maiden first-class victim, Michael Slater and Craig McDermott. During his nine years at Somerset his best performance was 80 with the bat and 7 for 23 with the ball. He moved to Derbyshire for one season but retired in 2002 after suffering a back injury. His first-class record was 1,693 runs at 21.98 and 129 wickets at 40.38.

After retiring he concentrated on qualifying as a coach, gaining experience at Bridgwater C.C. before his appointment as Somerset Academy Director in 2006. After acting as First Eleven bowling coach he became Head Coach in 2017 working under Director of Cricket Andy Hurry as they both strive to win the elusive Championship title for the first time.

Inns	Runs	HS	Ave	50/100	Balls	Runs	Wkts	BB	Ave	5w/10w	Ct
95	1693	80	21.98	8/0	8074	5210	129	7-23	40.38	2/0	18

LIST A											
Inns	Runs	HS	Ave	50/100	Balls	Runs	Wkts	BB	Ave	4w/5w	Ct
77	769	65*	13.25	2/0	4379	3730	124	4-28	30.08	1/0	18

Matthew Taylor

RHB/SLA
b. 13th November 1973, Bolton
Career 1994, 4 matches
List A: 2000, 2 matches (for Lancashire Cricket Board)
Debut: Derbyshire v Glamorgan, Cardiff, 16th June 1994
HS: 14* Derbyshire v Lancashire, Blackpool 1994
BB: 3-25 Derbyshire v New Zealand, Derby 1994

MATTHEW TAYLOR was born in Bolton on 13th November 1973. He first played for British Aerospace C.C. before moving to Horwich C.C. and impressed as a slow left arm bowler and useful right hand bat. He was soon involved with Lancashire youth representative teams playing for the very strong side that won the NatWest Trophy at Taunton School in 1988 and the following year he took 3 for 9 as Lancashire under 15's bowled Surrey out for 69 to gain a memorable victory at The Oval.

In 1990 Matthew displayed his bowling skills for the formidable Lancashire team that won the national Texaco Under 16's County Championship title. I notice that in an early trial game against the North of England under 15's team at Burnley C.C. he

Matthew Taylor playing for Derbyshire against Lancashire at Stanley Park, Blackpool on 18th July 1994.

dismissed the future England captain Michael Vaughan for 36 and also that a future England footballer Gary Neville was batting at number six. His best performance was against Durham in a very close quarter-final at Chorley C.C. where his excellent spell of 5 for 58 swung the game in Lancashire's favour to claim victory by 13 runs. In the finals at Uppingham School, Lancashire won all three matches very easily and ended the season with a perfect record having won all 13 played. It was indeed a vintage year.

From 1991 to 1993 Matthew played representative cricket for the Lancashire Federation under 19 team enjoying his best season in his final year as he operated in tandem with off spinner Chris Brown of Werneth C.C. Lancashire won the Cambridge Festival final when they beat Essex by 23 runs with the pair bowling 53 of the 60 overs and taking nine wickets. The team had earned the right to play Durham, the Oxford Festival winners, in a play-off final at Christ Church College. A poor batting performance gave Lancashire a total of only 159 but it was enough as Durham were dismissed for 83 with Matthew taking 5 for 19. Lancashire had won the overall Festivals Trophy and Matthew was declared 'Man of the Match' and was soon to discover that Derbyshire were prepared to offer him a contract for the 1994 season.

In his one and only first-class summer he played in three County Championship matches for Derbyshire making his debut against Glamorgan at Cardiff with David Hemp as his first victim and overall figures of 3 for 56 in 33 overs. In his next appearance he became part of cricket history when he was the last man dismissed by Middlesex fast bowler Richard Johnson as he recorded figures of 10 for 45, the first bowler to take all ten since Ian Thomson of Sussex thirty years earlier. His final taste of county cricket was against his native Lancashire at Blackpool in an amazing game which Derbyshire won by three wickets. After declaring at 490 for 8, Derbyshire dismissed Lancashire for 83 as Phil DeFreitas with 6 for 39 and Devon Malcolm with 4 for 43 tore through the order. Set to make 186 for victory, after Lancashire had made a much better fist of it second time round, Derbyshire reached their target with seven wickets down and one over to spare. For the most part of the game Matthew had not been too involved but he did take the important wicket of Neil Fairbrother. He was released at the end of the season having taken 7 wickets at 29.28 and scored 25 runs at 8.33 in four first-class games.

He continued to play some Second Eleven cricket for Lancashire and became professional at Moorside C.C. in the Saddleworth League before moving to Adlington C.C. where he was professional from 1997 to 2004. He was a great success taking 685 wickets and scoring 3,300 runs. On three occasions he claimed 100 wickets in the season and there is no doubt he was a fine league cricketer who was well respected in the Bolton area.

Inns	Runs	HS	Ave	50/100	Balls	Runs	Wkts	BB	Ave	5w/10w	Ct
5	25	14*	8.33	0/0	493	205	7	3-25	29.28	0/0	0

LIST A											
Inns	Runs	HS	Ave	50/100	Balls	Runs	Wkts	BB	Ave	4w/5w	Ct
1	5	5	5.00	0/0	120	52	1	1-22	52.00	0/0	2

Michael Powell

RHB/RM
b. 5th April 1975, Bolton
Career 1996-2008, 149 matches
List A 1999-2008, 118 matches
T20 2005-2008, 24 matches
Debut: Warwickshire v Durham, Edgbaston, 8th August 1996
HS: 236 Warwickshire v Oxford University Centre of Cricketing Excellence,
The Parks 2001
BB: 2-16 Warwickshire v Oxford University, The Parks 1998

MICHAEL JAMES POWELL was born in Bolton on 5th April 1975 and as a youngster was coached by Dave Fairbrother and played cricket for British Aerospace C.C. in the Bolton Association. His family moved to the Midlands where he attended Lawrence Sheriff School, Rugby and was soon involved with Warwickshire youth cricket. In 1990 he played for the Warwickshire under 16 team in the Texaco Trophy finals at Uppingham School, opening the batting against Lancashire, the eventual champions, and was dismissed cheaply by Andrew Payne. Nevertheless he was rated highly and good enough to captain England under 18's on their tours to South Africa in 1992/93 and

Denmark in 1993. He also represented England under 19's on the tour to Sri Lanka in 1993/94 alongside Michael Vaughan (captain), Gary Keedy, Chris Schofield and Nathan Wood.

Michael was medium in build and a solid right hand top order batsman capable of playing defiantly for long periods as demonstrated in his final innings for the county when scoring 68 not out from 213 balls to save the team from defeat. He made his county debut in 1996 aged 21 and in 1998 became the first uncapped Warwickshire player for 49 years to carry his bat against Nottinghamshire at Edgbaston. He was capped the following year and in 2000 enjoyed his most successful season scoring 1,006 runs at 43.73 including two centuries. In 2001 he was selected as a replacement for the

England 'A' team tour to the West Indies, scoring 340 runs at 34.00 with a top score of 96 against Barbados in an opening stand of 224 with Ian Ward. Much to his surprise he was appointed captain of Warwickshire for the 2001 season.

Warwickshire had enjoyed a great deal of success in the mid 1990's and were going through a period of transition so Michael knew he was taking on a difficult task. Nevertheless he tackled it head on and led the side to promotion in the Championship in 2001 and the following year second place in the First Division plus B&H Cup glory at Lord's. He had proved to be a strong and popular captain working closely with Bob Woolmer, the Director of Coaching, and producing favourable results. However his batting form had slumped, which was understandable when he had taken on such responsibility at the age of 25 and after playing only 44 first-class games. In his third year in charge the team finished fifth in Division One but Woolmer had moved on and although he scored 686 runs at 32.66, Michael decided to stand down citing bad form. Nick Knight was appointed, the sixth captain in the last nine seasons.

Michael continued to play until the end of his benefit year in 2008 and left first-class cricket having scored 7,395 runs at 31.60 with 12 centuries. He became Director of Cricket/Housemaster at Loretto School, Edinburgh from 2008-2014 before moving back to the Midlands where he is currently director of Cricket and an Assistant House Master at Rugby School.

Inns	Runs	HS	Ave	50/100	Balls	Runs	Wkts	BB	Ave	5w/10w	Ct
246	7395	236	31.60	12/40	1320	745	11	2-16	67.72	0/0	105

LIST A											
Inns	Runs	HS	Ave	50/100	Balls	Runs	Wkts	BB	Ave	4w/5w	Ct
99	2118	101*	25.82	5/1	824	727	25	5-40	29.08	0/1	56

T20											
Inns	Runs	HS	Ave	50/100	Balls	Runs	Wkts	BB	Ave	4w/5w	Ct
18	264	44*	22.00	0/0	-	-	-	-	-	-	10

Saj Mahmood

RHB/RFM
b. 21st December 1981, Bolton
Career 2002-2014, 121 matches
List A 2001-2013, 153 matches
T20 2003-2012, 69 matches
Debut v Hampshire, Old Trafford, 8th August 2002
HS: 94 v Sussex, Old Trafford 2004
BB: 6-30 v Durham, Chester-le-Street 2009
Tests: 8, 2006-2006/07
HS: 34 v Pakistan, Headingley 2006
BB: 4-22 v Pakistan, Headingley 2006
ODI: 26, 2004-2009/10
HS: 22* v Pakistan, Edgbaston 2006
BB: 4-50 v Sri Lanka, Antigua (ICC World Cup) 2006/7
International T20: 4, 2006-2009/10
HS: 1* v South Africa, Johannesburg 2009/10
BB: 1-31 v South Africa, Centurion 2009/10

SAJID IQBAL MAHMOOD was born in Bolton on 21st December 1981 after his family had emigrated to Lancashire from Rawalpindi in Pakistan in 1968. His cousin is the boxer Amir Khan who was also a useful cricketer and they grew up close together and still remain great friends.

Sajid, 6 foot 4 inches tall and strongly built, first showed his fast bowling ability playing for Astley Bridge C.C. and Egerton C.C. in the Bolton League and was offered a scholarship deal by Lancashire in 2002. He made his county debut against Hampshire the same year in a rain-affected game at Old Trafford and was soon offered a full contract. He made rapid progress in 2003, winning the Denis Compton award for the most promising young Lancashire player of the season and gaining selection for the ECB National Academy during the winter. Despite having taken only six first-class wickets Sajid was fast-tracked onto the England 'A' tour of India and Malaysia in 2003/04 emerging as a *"quality performer and strong England candidate"* according to *Wisden*.

He made his Test debut in 2006 against Sri Lanka at Lord's and had a spectacular start taking three wickets in his first 9 balls and two more wickets in the second innings. He played a further four Tests throughout the summer with his most successful return at Headingley against Pakistan, scoring 34 and taking 4 for 22 as England won comfortably. The final game of the series at The Oval was infamous for the fact that Pakistan refused to take the field after being accused of ball tampering and England were awarded the match.

In 2006-07 he was included in the touring party to Australia with Andrew Flintoff as captain and James Anderson also in the squad. Sadly England suffered a total whitewash in their quest for the Ashes. Although the final match at Sydney was lost by ten wickets it was notable as one of the rare occasions when one county has provided three fast bowlers for England in an Ashes Test as Flintoff, Anderson and Mahmood took the field. It was Sajid's final taste of Test cricket and he moved on having taken 20 wickets at 38.10 and scored 81 runs at 8.10.

England did not return home in total shame however, as they pulled themselves together beating Australia three times to win the One-Day Commonwealth Bank Trophy with Sajid bowling steadily. He retained his place in the World Cup squad in 2007 winning the 'Man of the Match' award against Bangladesh and playing his final One-Day International against South Africa in 2009. In his 26 match ODI career he had captured 30 wickets at 38.94 and scored 85 runs at 7.72.

In Championship cricket Sajid's most successful season was 2009 with 38 wickets and although he showed some talent with the bat in his early days, scoring a career-best 94 against Sussex at Old Trafford, he did not really fulfil his promise apart from one season in 2010 when he totalled 564 runs at an average of 31.33. His self-confessed favourite year was 2011 when Lancashire won the Championship outright for the first time since 1934. It turned out to be the only trophy the county won in his Red Rose days. He played in 10 of the 16 matches during that momentous season with a standout performance against Nottinghamshire at Trent Bridge, taking five wickets in each innings. His overall figures were 35 wickets at 29.90 and 256 runs at 17.07, and he had played an important role in what was very much an outstanding team triumph.

After appearing in only three Championship fixtures in 2012 Sajid ended the season on loan at Somerset. He had been an exciting and talented player with his pace, aggression and ability to surprise batsmen but younger pace bowlers were beginning to make their mark and his form had started to dip. He would be missed in the dressing room for his humour and practical jokes but he was leaving with a much prized outright Championship medal which not even the legendary Brian Statham could claim.

He signed for Essex for the 2013 and 2014 seasons but experienced little success before retiring with a first-class career record of 329 wickets at 32.82 and 2,178 runs at 15.78 from his 121 appearances. He returned to the north to play league cricket and became involved in a clothing business for a time before moving to the London area. He has recently passed the Level 2 Cricket Coaching Course and instructs underprivileged young people how to play the game at the William Perkin C of E High School in Ealing.

Inns	Runs	HS	Ave	50/100	Balls	Runs	Wkts	BB	Ave	5w/10w	Ct
158	2178	94	15.78	10/0	17204	10802	329	6-30	32.83	9/2	30

LIST A											
Inns	Runs	HS	Ave	50/100	Balls	Runs	Wkts	BB	Ave	4w/5w	Ct
82	541	29	9.16	0/0	6683	5985	210	5-16	28.50	7/1	23

T20											
Inns	Runs	HS	Ave	50/100	Balls	Runs	Wkts	BB	Ave	4w/5w	Ct
31	183	34	7.95	0/0	1450	1920	77	4-21	24.93	2/0	18

Karl Brown

RHB/RMF
b. 17th May 1988, Bolton
Career 2006-2018, 85 matches
List A 2007-2018, 80 matches
T20 2011-2018, 91 matches
Debut v Durham Centre of Cricketing Excellence, Durham, 10th May 2006
HS: 132 v Warwickshire, Old Trafford 2015
BB: 2-30 v Nottinghamshire, Old Trafford 2009

KARL ROBERT BROWN was born in Bolton on 17th May 1988. His father Paul was a good player at Atherton C.C. and it was there that Karl first showed his exceptional talent for the club's under 11 team. He was good enough to be selected for the Lancashire under 11 team a year early and scored a magnificent 71 not out at the Kent Festival. By the age of fifteen he was opening the batting regularly for the Atherton C.C. first team and the following year became the youngest player in the long history of the Bolton Association to score over 1,000 runs in a season as he recorded 1,115 with an average of 42.12. Furthermore he hit the headlines for Lancashire Schools at various age groups resulting in his selection for England at under 15, under 16, under 17 and under 19 levels.

It was a stellar start to his cricket career and he was rewarded by being selected for the first intake of the Lancashire Academy in 2003 alongside future county players Steven Croft, Tom Smith, Steven Mullaney and John Simpson. He was awarded a Lancashire contract in 2006 and made his first-class debut against Durham University early in the new season. It was 2008 before he made his Championship debut but Karl had only appeared in half a dozen further games before the memorable 2011 season began. What lay ahead was probably his most enjoyable and satisfying season at Old Trafford as he took on the responsibility of batting at number three throughout the campaign.

He immediately stepped up to the mark in the first match of the season against Sussex at Aigburth as he registered his maiden century and it was somehow rather fitting that Karl and Steven Croft, two of the many home grown lads in the squad, were batting together at Taunton when the winning runs were scored and the Championship was won outright for the first time since 1934. Karl had done exactly what was required of him, playing solidly and consistently in all 16 matches with an aggregate of 888 runs at an average of 34.15. He was 'over the moon' that afternoon in Taunton as were all the other players and supporters as they celebrated the dream conclusion to a Championship season. Karl was soon informed that he was named in the England Performance programme squad to tour Sri Lanka in the winter and at the end of season awards night at Old Trafford he was also voted 'Lancashire Young Player of the Year'.

Karl Brown and Steven Croft leave the field after the partnership which secured Lancashire's first outright Championship trophy for 77 years.

2011 had been very much a breakthrough season for Karl and there were high expectations of him at both county and international level. In the following three Championship seasons, however, he was unable to make progress, scoring just over a thousand runs and averaging in the early 20's in 32 games. In 2015 hopes were again raised as a return to form brought him 766 runs at an average of 45.05 resulting in the awarding of his county cap. The fact that he only made 12 more Championship appearances tells its own story and although he continued to perform well in 50-over and T20 competitions he was not re-engaged after the 2018 season. His first-class record was 3,572 runs including two centuries at an average of 26.65 in 85 games and a more impressive one-day record of 2,420 runs including two centuries at an average of 37.81.

He departed with a much treasured County Championship winner's medal and also a T20 Blast winner's medal following Lancashire's success in 2015. He had served his county well and loved his time as a professional cricketer. He was immediately signed by Accrington C.C. as professional for the 2019 season and was also appointed Cricket Coach at Cheadle Hulme School.

Inns	Runs	HS	Ave	50/100	Balls	Runs	Wkts	BB	Ave	5w/10w	Ct
140	3572	132	26.65	22/2	90	65	2	2-30	32.50	0/0	52

LIST A											
Inns	Runs	HS	Ave	50/100	Balls	Runs	Wkts	BB	Ave	4w/5w	Ct
76	2420	129	37.81	14/2	6	17	0	0-17	-	0/0	21

T20											
Inns	Runs	HS	Ave	50/100	Balls	Runs	Wkts	BB	Ave	4w/5w	Ct
88	2188	69	27.69	16/0	-	-	-	-	-	-	30

Haseeb Hameed

RHB/LB
b. 17th January 1997, Bolton
Career 2015-2019, 63 matches
List A 2017-2019, 19 matches
Debut v Glamorgan, Old Trafford, 21st August 2015
HS: 122 v Nottinghamshire, Trent Bridge 2016
BB: 0-0 v Surrey, The Oval 2017
Test: 3, 2016/17
HS: 82 v India, Rajkot 2016/17
Did not bowl

HASEEB HAMEED was born in Bolton on 17th January 1997. His parents had emigrated from India to the north of England and Ismail, his father, had played league cricket and coached his youngest son very well from an early age. In fact Haseeb was first discovered aged eight by John Roberts, the well-known local cricketer and coach, as he practised in the nets with his father at Tonge C.C. in the Bolton League.

The following year he was selected for the Lancashire Schools under 11 team at the age of nine after impressing manager John Charlson in early trials. Although he was not very powerful, Haseeb demonstrated great technical ability and potential for the future by scoring over 300 runs. Twelve months later he registered his first century against Kent and in his final season, playing for both the county under 11 and under 12 teams, really made a bold statement by scoring 811 runs with an average of 90. Such high scoring at this level had not been witnessed since the days of Andrew Flintoff.

When he was thirteen Haseeb went to Bolton School where he played for the same team as Callum and Matthew Parkinson and all three helped to bring great kudos to the school as the cricket team won the English Schools Cricket Association/ECB T20 national trophy. In the final against Whitgift School Haseeb demonstrated his class by scoring 83 not out in a ten-wicket victory. It was the first time a northern school had won this prestigious trophy.

At this stage of his career Haseeb was very involved at Bolton School, Lancashire Schools and club levels and had left Tonge to join Farnworth Social Circle C.C. where he teamed up with Josh Bohannon for a few years before moving to Formby C.C. in the Liverpool Competition. The county coaches were well aware of his precocious talent and selected him for the Lancashire Academy at the age of fifteen.

He continued to excel in all age groups after his remarkable start in the Lancashire under 11 team and won trophies at under 14, under 15 and under 17 levels. He also gained international honours playing for England at under 15, under 17 and under 19 age groups where he captained the side aged 18 and produced scores of 92, 112, 97, 97 and 125 in consecutive innings. He signed professional terms for Lancashire at the end of the 2014 season at the same time as his fellow youth internationals Matthew Parkinson and Saqib Mahmood.

After taking his 'A' level exams in 2015 Haseeb was available to play more Second Eleven cricket and performed so well that he was promoted to the first team, making his County Championship debut against Glamorgan at Old Trafford in late August. He opened the batting with Karl Brown and shared a 76-run partnership, scoring 28 and retaining his place for the final three games in which he averaged 42 with a highest score of 91 against Surrey at Old Trafford. It was a confident start showing composure, a good technique and judgement befitting a seasoned campaigner. Lancashire finished runners-up in division two of the Championship and were promoted back to the top flight for 2016. In making his debut Haseeb became the fourth former pupil of Bolton School to play for Lancashire after Donny Davies, Jack Bond and Duncan Worsley. Within twelve months his school colleagues Matthew Parkinson and his twin brother Callum also made their Championship debuts although Callum's was for Derbyshire.

Haseeb relished the new and more demanding challenge of first division cricket as he shattered expectations and created one record after another. He was often likened to a young Michael Atherton as he displayed a calm maturity and uncanny ability to judge line and length. Furthermore he knew how to pace an innings and minimise risk and after his majestic display in the Roses Match at Old Trafford the seasoned Yorkshire captain Andrew Gale remarked that, "Haseeb is one of the best young players I've seen in a long time."

During his remarkable summer of 2016 Haseeb created many new records. In the Yorkshire game mentioned above he became the first Lancastrian to score two centuries in a Roses match although two Yorkshire players had accomplished the feat. He also became the youngest Lancashire player to

score 1,000 runs in a first-class season, the youngest from any county to score two centuries in a first-class match and the first teenage opener to make four centuries in a Championship season. He was duly awarded his county cap by Lancashire Chairman Michael Cairns during the Middlesex match at Old Trafford. After enjoying such an incredible summer it was hardly a surprise when the England selectors decided to back his class and picked him in the squad to tour Bangladesh and India during the winter.

At 19 years and 297 days Haseeb broke yet another record when he became England's youngest Test opener when making his debut against India in Rajkot. He considered it amazing that he made his first Test appearance in the state of Gujarat where his parents were born. Only Brian Close, Jack Crawford, Denis Compton, and Ben Hollioake were younger Test debutants for England. In his first Test he opened with Alastair Cook and played like a veteran, leaving the ball well and looking very assured in defence. He scored 31 in the first innings but was more positive in the second as he struck a classy 82 in a first wicket partnership of 180 with his captain. In the second Test he was run out unfortunately for 13 but in the second innings demonstrated his determination to fight in adverse conditions against Ravi Ashwin and Ravi Jadeja scoring 25 as he and Cook defended for more than 50 overs in a partnership of 75. In Mohali England needed to win to square the series but lost by eight wickets and Haseeb was unfortunate to suffer a broken finger which ended his tour.He was hit on the left hand little finger by Umesh Yadav as he was dismissed for 9 on the first day but, coming in to bat at number 8 on the fourth day, he played with great courage and skill to make a valiant 59 not out. His introduction to Test cricket at the age of 19 had been a great success as he scored 219 runs at 43.80 in his six innings. He had displayed calmness, acumen, a sound technique and not least bravery in difficult circumstances. Everyone, including Virat Kohli and Sachin Tendulkar, was impressed and he looked certain to become a fixture in the England team for years to come.

It is very disappointing and something of a mystery that Haseeb has not been able to recapture his amazing form of 2016. He has certainly not batted with his usual composure and sound judgement since breaking a finger in India. On returning to Old Trafford he experienced an average summer in 2017 making 513 runs at 28.50 followed by a season best forgotten. There is no definitive answer to his problems and it has happened to many cricketers in the past but I am sure he has been offered words of encouragement and advice from his coaches and fellow professionals. He has suffered a difficult couple of years but he is a fighter and deserves a change of fortune. After starting the 2019 season with a double century against Loughborough MCCU and an accomplished 117 against Middlesex at Lord's, Haseeb was sadly unable to maintain the form that many Lancastrians craved. He only recorded one half century during the ten other Championship games in which he played and the county decided not to offer him a new contract.

In November 2019 Haseeb signed a two-year deal with Nottinghamshire and will work with the former Red Rose and England coach Peter Moores. There is no doubting Haseeb's talent and temperament and at the age of 22 he still has a good chance of recapturing the form to succeed at the highest level. On becoming a Notts player Haseeb stated, "this is a new chapter in both my life and career" and although many Lancashire followers are sorry to see him leave perhaps it is the best move for him to have made to kick start his form. I sincerely hope that is the case.

Inns	Runs	HS	Ave	50/100	Balls	Runs	Wkts	BB	Ave	5w/10w	Ct
106	2907	122	30.60	15/5	42	21	0	0-00	-	0/0	35

LIST A											
Inns	Runs	HS	Ave	50/100	Balls	Runs	Wkts	BB	Ave	4w/5w	Ct
19	556	88	34.75	4/0	-	-	-	-	-	-	3

Matt Parkinson

RHB/LB
b. 24th October 1996, Bolton
Career 2016-2019, 20 matches
List A 2017/18-2019, 25 matches
T20 2017-2019 38 matches
Debut v Warwickshire, Old Trafford, 20th June 2016
HS: 14 v Middlesex, Old Trafford 2019
BB: 6-23 v Sussex, Old Trafford 2019
ODI: 2, 2020
BB: 0-15 v South Africa, Durban 2020
Did not bat
International T20: 2 matches, 2019
BB: 4-47 v New Zealand, Napier 2019
Did not bat

MATTHEW WILLIAM PARKINSON was born in Bolton on 24th October 1996 and he is the twin brother of Callum who plays county cricket for Leicestershire C.C.C. His father David was a leg break bowler in the Bolton League and it was under his guidance at Heaton C.C. that Matthew started to learn the difficult skills of wrist spin when he was eight or nine years old. He batted and bowled right handed, was extremely enthusiastic and always wanted to be in the action. He attended Bolton School from the age of seven and by the time he was ten had earned a place in the Lancashire Schools under 11 team alongside his twin brother. It was at this early stage of his cricket career that he started to play with other very talented boys in the same team. It is hardly surprising that national titles were won at under 14, under 15 and under 17 levels with a team that included, in addition to the Parkinson twins, Haseeb Hameed, Josh Bohannon and Harry Dearden, all future county players, as well as Bradley Yates and Callum Turner who have both played for the Lancashire Second Eleven.

Matthew was in great demand playing representative cricket but also managed to figure prominently in the Bolton School under 15 team that won the ESCA/ECB T20 Trophy in the National Cricket Final at Arundel

Castle in 2012. In the semi-final Shrewsbury School made 154 for 8 and Bolton made a poor start losing three early and important wickets but Matthew displayed his ability with the bat in making an aggressive and game changing 87 not out to ensure victory. In the final against a talented Whitgift School team he bowled skilfully to take four wickets for 17 runs, helping to restrict Whitgift to 133 for 8 which Bolton reached comfortably without losing a wicket thanks to Haseeb Hameed and his brother Callum.

To win such a prestigious trophy was a great team achievement as over one thousand schools had entered the competition countrywide, and it was the first time a northern school had accomplished the feat. Bolton School and master in charge of cricket Andy Compton are rightly very proud of this outstanding success.

At club level Matthew was making good progress at Heaton but decided to move to Urmston C.C. in the Cheshire County League at the age of fourteen and a few years later was invited to play Minor Counties cricket for Staffordshire. He had also been selected for the Lancashire Academy aged fifteen and made his Lancashire Second Eleven debut the following year. He signed professional terms with Lancashire in 2015 and also played four matches for England under 19's including a four-day Test against Australia at Durham where he took six wickets in the first innings and three wickets in the second.

In 2016 Matthew made a spectacular debut for Lancashire against Warwickshire at Old Trafford. He had only bowled three balls of his first over when a loud, disturbing noise from the PA system forced the players to leave the field for thirty minutes and take an early tea. On returning Matthew immediately dismissed the seasoned Test batsman Jonathan Trott for his maiden Championship wicket and the following day finished off the tail to end with the excellent figures of 5 for 49 from 23 overs. He had kept his head and bowled with turn and accuracy to become only the second leg spinner after Adil Rashid to take five wickets on debut since the end of the war.

Matthew was voted Lancashire Young Player of the Year in 2017 as he made a breakthrough in T20 cricket taking 14 wickets in nine appearances and also demonstrating impressive control with an excellent economy rate of 6.06, one of the best in the competition. In 2018 he continued to succeed in T20 cricket and also became a force in the 50-over Royal London Cup as he was leading wicket taker in the competition, winning both the One-Day and Young Player of the Year awards. He only played in six Championship games, taking 16 wickets, but managed another five wicket haul against Somerset at Old Trafford. In the winter he unfortunately suffered an injury which prevented him from taking up a lucrative contract to play T20 cricket in Australia.

By the summer of 2019 he was fit again and raring to impress. During the course of the season he again bowled well in the One-Day Cup and was the third most successful bowler with 21 wickets at an average of 14.61 in the T20 Blast, no other bowler having taken more wickets in the last three years. He also recorded a career-best match analysis of 10 for 165 against Sussex at Old Trafford and was awarded his county cap by Chairman David Hodgkiss in August. It was during the final Championship match of the season against Leicestershire at Grace Road that Matthew was informed by Steven Croft that he had been selected for the England tour to New Zealand and he no doubt celebrated with his brother Callum who was playing for Leicestershire. The match will be remembered for the fact that the twins dismissed each other in the same first-class match which had never happened before.

Matthew and Callum's mother Maria very sadly died during the summer but how proud she and David, their father, would have been to see Matthew playing in his first senior international game for England. Both parents had given wonderful support to their sons' cricket activities from a very early age even to the extent of creating an indoor practice area in their home.

Matthew made his debut for England in the third T20 match against New Zealand at Nelson in November 2019. He displayed great composure in a very tidy two over spell costing 14 runs and taking the wicket of Tim Seifert. England lost the match but fought back strongly in the 4th game at Napier to win by 76 runs with Matthew keeping a steady head and getting the ball above the batsman's eye-line to claim 4 for 47 on a ground with short boundaries. He was not selected for the deciding match in the series which England won, but he had made a good impression and played an important part in the success of the development team against an almost full strength New Zealand side.

Although Matthew was not selected for either of the two Test matches in New Zealand he will have gained some valuable experience, and was included in the squad for the winter tour to South Africa where he made his one-day international debut and included in the subsequent Test squad for the tour to Sri Lanka.

I am sure he will realise that 2020 is an important year for both himself and the county club to further develop and demonstrate that they can compete at the highest level.

Inns	Runs	HS	Ave	50/100	Balls	Runs	Wkts	BB	Ave	5w/10w	Ct
26	90	14	5.29	0/0	3029	1564	62	6-23	25.22	3/1	6

LIST A											
Inns	Runs	HS	Ave	50/100	Balls	Runs	Wkts	BB	Ave	4w/5w	Ct
11	43	15*	14.33	0/0	1367	1178	42	5-51	28.05	2/2	4

T20											
Inns	Runs	HS	Ave	50/100	Balls	Runs	Wkts	BB	Ave	4w/5w	Ct
7	14	7*	4.66	0/0	814	977	65	4 23	15.03	3/0	5

Callum Parkinson

RHB/SLA
b. 24th October 1996, Bolton
Career 2016-2019, 25 matches
List A 2017-2019, 13 matches
T20 2017-2019 43 matches
Debut: Derbyshire v Leicestershire, Leicester, 4th August 2016
HS: 75 v Kent, Canterbury 2017
BB: 8-148 v Worcestershire, Worcester 2017

Photo courtesy of Luke Adams.

CALLUM FRANCIS PARKINSON was born in Bolton on 24th October 1996 and he is the twin brother of Matthew who plays for Lancashire C.C.C. Their father David was a leg spin bowler in the Bolton League and introduced his sons to the game at Heaton C.C. when they were very young. The twins attended Bolton School Junior Dept. from the age of seven and Callum was selected for the Lancashire Schools under 11 team a year early as a right hand bat and fast left arm bowler. He immediately impressed by taking ten wickets in his first season and the following year he was good enough to open both the batting and bowling. He had made great strides by the age of eleven making his first century against Cheshire and scoring 431 runs overall. He continued his successful run in 2009 with some excellent all-round performances for

Lancashire under 12's claiming a total of 24 wickets and 297 runs, and he followed up with a further 360 runs at under 14 level.

Callum was a very talented and enthusiastic young cricketer and was in great demand at school, club and representative levels. It is one of the dilemmas that parents of gifted young cricketers face trying to decide where and when their children should play and it is further complicated by having to juggle the travel arrangements. They somehow get round these problems however and there is no doubt that without their co-operation the present programme of cricket fixtures would not be possible. It is fortunate that most parents enjoy the game of cricket and I am sure it has given them a great deal of enjoyment as they support their children, travelling to different grounds and making new friends.

In his mid-teens Callum, now a slow left arm bowler, was beginning to experience first team cricket for Heaton but soon moved to Urmston C.C. in the Cheshire County League and then Staffordshire to sample Minor Counties cricket. Along the way he had continued to taste success winning national Championships for some very strong Lancashire junior teams at under 14, under 15 and under 17 age groups. In 2012 he was a member of the Bolton School under 15 team that became the first northern school to win the English Schools Cricket Association/ECB T20 Trophy in the National Cricket Final at Arundel Castle in Sussex. Chasing a total of 133 for 8, Callum opened the batting with Haseeb Hameed and they reached the target without loss, Callum scoring 41 and Haseeb 83.

Unlike his brother, Callum was not selected for the Lancashire Academy but was invited to join the Derbyshire Academy in 2016 and quickly made his County Championship debut against Leicestershire at Grace Road in the same year. His twin Matthew had made his debut for Lancashire two months earlier taking five wickets in the first innings, and Callum also did well, scoring 48 not out and taking 7 for 178 in the match. He had impressed the opposition and, after playing three more games for Derbyshire, was offered a contract for the 2017 season by Leicestershire.

He made his county debut for his new club against Kent at Grace Road but his best performance with the ball was later in the year against Worcestershire at New Road when he claimed 8 for 148 with *Wisden* stating: *'the considerable promise shown by left arm spinner Callum Parkinson was exciting'* and that he had *'outbowled Indian Test star Ravichandran Ashwin'* on a turning pitch. He also figured prominently as a batsman against Kent at Canterbury making 75 in a last wicket partnership of 122 with Lewis Hill which created a new record between the sides. Callum had made a very promising start with both bat and ball in his five Championship appearances but his performances in 2018 were rather disappointing. It is very important to remember, however, that T20 and 50-over cricket feature prominently in the modern game and Leicestershire have recognised this fact by extending a talented young cricketer's contract to the end of 2020.

Inns	Runs	HS	Ave	50/100	Balls	Runs	Wkts	BB	Ave	5w/10w	Ct
39	593	75	18.53	1/0	3730	2148	46	8-148	46.69	1/1	4

LIST A

Inns	Runs	HS	Ave	50/100	Balls	Runs	Wkts	BB	Ave	4w/5w	Ct
11	222	52*	27.75	1/0	552	589	4	1-34	147.25	0/0	2

T20

Inns	Runs	HS	Ave	50/100	Balls	Runs	Wkts	BB	Ave	4w/5w	Ct
22	146	27*	12.16	0/0	804	1048	42	4-20	24.95	1/0	6

Josh Bohannon

RHB/SLA
b. 9th April 1997, Bolton
Career 2018-2019, 16 matches
List A 2018-2019, 15 matches
T20 2018-2019 14 matches
Debut v Surrey, The Oval, 19th August 2018
HS: 174 v Derbyshire, Old Trafford 2019
BB: 3-46 v Hampshire, Southampton 2018

JOSHUA JAMES BOHANNON was born in Bolton on 9th April 1997. He attended Harper Green High School where another Lancashire all-rounder Steven O'Shaughnessy had been a pupil. He joined his local cricket club Farnworth Social Circle at a young age and there developed his skills as a right handed batsman and right arm seam bowler who was also an outstanding fielder. In 2008 he was selected for the Lancashire under 11 team and made a good start scoring 192 runs in the season followed by 227 for the county under 12 team a year later. Already Josh was displaying immense talent and a wonderful attitude to the game, never giving anything less than one hundred percent effort.

He continued to develop well at club and also representative level where he won trophies playing for Lancashire at under 14, under 15 and under 17 age groups. In 2014 he had an outstanding season and was voted Young Lancashire Cricketer of the Year. His consistent performances for the formidable trophy-winning under 17 team started with a century against Durham followed by a match-winning 60 against Cheshire and an imperious double century against Staffordshire. He made his debut for the Lancashire Second Eleven aged 17 and was offered a place in the Academy in 2015 followed by a Scholarship in 2017. He was able to play more regularly scoring 471 runs for the Second Eleven including five fifties and was offered a full contract for the 2018 season.

Josh spent the winter of 2017-18 in Sydney playing for Randwick Petersham but suffered a side injury and missed the start of the English season. He worked very hard to regain fitness and performed well for the Second Eleven in all formats, even striking an eye-catching century in a T20 game at Old Trafford in front of the management. He made his 50-over debut against Warwickshire at Blackpool and a couple of months later his T20 debut against Leicestershire at Old Trafford. He was included in the first team for the last five Championship matches, starting in August with his first-class debut against Surrey at The Oval in difficult conditions under floodlights against South African pace bowler Morne Morkel with a pink ball. It was a tough audition

Josh Bohannon celebrates his maiden first-class century.

but Josh stepped up to the mark scoring 52 in the first innings as Lancashire lost narrowly by six runs. The following week at Southport he went one better, batting superbly in scoring 78 not out in a partnership of 139 with captain Dane Vilas as Lancashire beat Worcestershire by four wickets. It was certainly a memorable innings as it gave Lancashire a better chance of avoiding relegation, was achieved at the ground of a club where he had played some league cricket and also several family members were present to enjoy his success.

As it turned out Lancashire, despite a brave but belated attempt, were unfortunately unable to avoid relegation but Bohannon had made an impressive start and there were many signs that he has a bright future ahead. During a very successful 2019 season Lancashire gained immediate promotion as Champions of Division Two and remained undefeated throughout the season. They also challenged in the Royal London One-Day Cup reaching the semi-final and lost to Essex in the quarter-final of the T20 Blast in a match played at Durham because Old Trafford was unavailable.

Josh enjoyed an excellent season as he scored 472 runs at an average of 52.40 and cemented his place in the batting order moving from number 7 to number 3. In June he failed narrowly to record his maiden century scoring 98 not out against Leicestershire at Liverpool but in September at Old Trafford he rectified the situation in recording a splendid 174 against Derbyshire. He is a gifted batsman and fielder in all formats but will specially relish the opportunity to test himself against stronger opposition in a very competitive first division in 2020.

Inns	Runs	HS	Ave	50/100	Balls	Runs	Wkts	BB	Ave	5w/10w	Ct
21	727	174	42.76	4/1	820	468	10	3-46	46.80	0/0	6

LIST A

Inns	Runs	HS	Ave	50/100	Balls	Runs	Wkts	BB	Ave	4w/5w	Ct
10	210	55*	26.25	1/0	150	208	1	1-33	208.00	0/0	3

T20

Inns	Runs	HS	Ave	50/100	Balls	Runs	Wkts	BB	Ave	4w/5w	Ct
7	67	23	16.75	0/0	-	-			-	-	5

AUTHOR'S SELECTION

As is customary when writing a book such as this, I have put forward my own selection of players following the modern pattern of a squad of thirteen depending on conditions, form and fitness for the final eleven.

The thirteen I have chosen are:-

1. Charlie Hallows (Lancashire & England)
2. Dick Barlow (Lancashire & England)
3. Haseeb Hameed (Lancashire & England)
4. Duncan Worsley (Lancashire & Oxford University)
5. Jack Bond (Captain) (Lancashire)
6. Mike Watkinson (Lancashire & England)
7. James Hallows (Lancashire)
8. Bill Farrimond (wicketkeeper) (Lancashire & England)
9. Dick Tyldesley (Lancashire & England)
10. Frank Tyson (Northamptonshire & England)
11. Roy Tattersall (Lancashire & England)
12. Walter Brearley (Lancashire & England)
13. Dick Pollard (Lancashire & England)

Jack Bond is the standout captain and would bat at number five. The first four batsmen are solid and dependable but three have played Test cricket whilst Mike Watkinson and James Hallows are talented and versatile all-rounders and would bat at number six and seven. Bill Farrimond would keep wicket and bat at number eight followed by Frank Tyson who would lead the pace attack with either Walter Brearley or Dick Pollard. Brearley would be my first choice and I am confident Jack Bond would get the best out of him, but if he proved to be difficult Pollard would be a very worthy replacement. Roy Tattersall and Dick Tyldesley would form a formidable spin partnership in some matches which would mean the fast/medium attack would be in the hands of Tyson, Barlow, Watkinson and Hallows with Brearley and Pollard left out.

This squad leaves the captain with a bowling attack that possesses great skills, variety and depth including searing pace in Tyson and Brearley, medium pace expertise from Pollard, Barlow, Watkinson and Hallows and quality spin in Tattersall, Tyldesley, Watkinson and Hallows. There is clearly a lack of a quality stroke player in the top five but there is a great deal of dependability and application, and we are talking about the longer format of the game in any case. None of the players had an extended Test career but ten of them experienced international cricket and I am confident the side would acquit itself admirably in any imaginary inter-town competition in England - and especially against Reading!

Geoff Ogden

*The 'winter game' was a Boxing Day charity match held at Farnworth
Social Circle Cricket Club sometime in the 1960s.
Standing from left: Alan Hutchinson (Farnworth SC), Tommy Banks (BWFC and
England), Willie Moir (BWFC and Scotland), Jack Bond, Bill Taylor (Little Hulton).
Crouching are Brian Krikken (right) and behind the brazier
is Roland Gee (Farnworth).*

Where the book all began

The opening of the Clarendon Road Indoor Centre.
Bolton, 1956.
Duncan Worsley, Geoff Ogden, Jim Gledhill and The Mayor of Bolton.
The centre was very influential in developing Bolton cricketers.

Bibliography

Wisden Cricketers' Almanack
Cricket Archive
Lancashire Archive, Don Ambrose
Red Roses Crest The Caps, Eric Midwinter
From The Stretford End, Brian Bearshaw
Bolton League Handbook, Peter Stafford
Jack Bond – Lancashire Lad, Lancashire Leader, Douglas Miller
Cotton Town Cricket, Roy Cavanagh
Cricket in my Life, Arthur Hargreaves
A Who's Who of Lancashire C.C.C., Robert Brooke & David Goodyear
Lancashire C.C.C. 100 Greats, Keith Hayhurst
Champions....about bloomin' time!, Graham Hardcastle & Chris Ostick
Bolton C.C. – One Hundred Years at Green Lane, Mike McNeill & Roy Battersby
Inside The Boundary, Geoff Wellsteed